D0039151

UNVEILED

The Transforming Power of God's Presence and Voice

ALAN SMITH

Unveiled, The Transforming Power of God's Presence and Voice
Copyright © 2011 by Alan Smith

All rights reserved. No part of this publication may be reproduced, stored in a retrieval system, or transmitted in any form or by any means, electronic, mechanical, photocopying, or otherwise, without the prior written consent of the publisher. Short extracts may be used for review purposes.

Unless otherwise stated, all scripture quotations are taken from the English Standard Version (ESV):

The Holy Bible, English Standard Version* (ESV*)
Copyright © 2001 by Crossway,
a publishing ministry of Good News Publishers.
All rights reserved. ESV Text Edition: 2007

ISBN 978-1-4675-0348-8   North American edition
Library of Congress Control Number: 2011960908

Visit http://www.alansmithonline.com for additional ministry information.

Edited by Nancy Smith
Authority Press
Fort Worth, TX

Mountain Photograph by Abel Leemans
Cloud Photograph by Brandon Day
Layout & Cover Design by ThinkTree Media, LLC

Printed in the U.S.A.

For John Collins, who saw in me what I did not see.

Contents

Acknowledgements

I once heard a story about someone asking Jack Hayford how long it took him to prepare a sermon. He replied, "If I told you 'fifteen minutes', you wouldn't understand. If I told you 'forty years', you wouldn't understand that either." Though I've spent the last year doing it, in a very real sense, I've spent my whole life preparing to write this book, and hopefully others. That preparation has involved significant contributions from many. My hope is to express gratitude for some of those, though space will require me to exclude some, who, no doubt, merit mention.

Mom, you read the Bible to me every night throughout my childhood. You rose most mornings before the sun to meet alone with God. Your Bibles are worn and overly highlighted, margins filled with your thoughts and impressions. My name appears in the margins by many of those passages. You were praying for me. You still are. I am thankful.

Dad, you taught me about unconditional love. The sound of your melodic whistling as you walked up the sidewalk to pick me up for the weekend always made me feel valued. You taught me to love loud music, to dream big dreams, and to remain faithful in difficult circumstances. Thank you for your constant support and affirmation.

I've sat under the leadership and impartation of a group of wonderful pastors. Their faithfulness, example, instruction, support, and encouragement has significantly impacted my life. Thank you Doug White, Lee Bedford, Mark Morrow, Mark McKinney, John Collins, Jack & Alta Hatcher, Eric & Susan Hulet, and Jamey Miller for showing me how to love God, love others, and always smell like sheep in the process.

Jim Armstrong—You gave me your lenses. Thank you.

For the last several years I've had the privilege of serving with Bob Hamp, who has been my pastor, my mentor, my boss, and my friend. People say that I'm the other half of your brain. If that's true at all, it's one of the most honoring things that could ever be said of me. Thank you for including me in your journey.

Thank you Robert Morris and the leaders of Gateway Church. You have built a safe and healthy place for me and my family to grow and serve together. Being part of the ministry staff at Gateway is a constant adventure and an amazing privilege. Pastor Robert, your willingness to contribute the foreword is significant to me beyond words. Thank you.

Special thanks to Aja, Bob, Brady, Cathy, Julie, Katy, Linda, Michelle, Tracey, and Tommy for making Department 40 an incredible place to be everyday.

Todd Parks & Bill Sandford —Thank you for your investment in my life and future. I know there were others who helped. I'm grateful.

Many have mentored me through their writings: N.T. Wright, John Piper, Dallas Willard, Greg Boyd, Bill Johnson, C.S. Lewis, Francis Schaeffer, Norman Geisler, Watchman Nee, Dutch Sheets, and George Ladd, to name a few favorites. Though only occasionally cited in this work, their influence on the way I think flavors every page. That some of them might not appreciate being included with others on this list delights me to no end.

A small group of guys have made me rich in friendship: Jace Beasley, Steve Billingsley, Robb Brewer, Edward Jones, Julian Kindred, and Jon Pignatelli. I love you.

Judy, Christyl, Laura, Candice, Dan, and Jay—thank you for praying.

Several friends were kind enough to read my manuscript and provide helpful feedback. George Thomas, Cheri Cochran, Bob Hamp, Lenore Ludlow, Joanna Wiesinger, Erica Flynn, Laura Mantey, Paige Henderson, Steve Billingsley, Jamey Miller, Jeff Jenkins, Allan Kelsey, Erica LeBlanc, and Yuri Star. Thank you for your investment of time and love.

David and Jill Routzon—Thank you for accepting me. I needed it.

Lauren, Anna, and Teddy—I delight in you. Being your

dad is proof that God loves me and wants me to be happy. Thanks for your patience and love during this season. My wife of seventeen years, Nancy, has assumed a new role in my life during this project: *editor*. You've always honored, encouraged, cheered, celebrated, and loved me. In this process, you've also had to correct me, which I needed. You've done it with the same beauty, grace, and intelligence you bring to every aspect of our lives. I love that what we are called to do is beginning to overlap and intersect in these ways. It reminds me of heaven and earth. Thank you.

Foreword

As a pastor, I am passionate about teaching God's truth to my congregation. However, I don't want them to only hear truth and forget it all when they leave church. I want to speak from my own experiences with God in a way that encourages others to have *their* own experiences with Him.

Over the years at Gateway Church, I've made a conscious effort to surround myself with anointed individuals who share that same goal. That's why I was so happy when Alan Smith joined our church staff as one of our pastors. Alan understands that there's no greater privilege in life than knowing God. This is evident in his life, his ministry, his teaching and now his book. Alan is an expert at taking big ideas and making them understandable and relatable without watering them down.

This talent serves him so well in this book. God's presence is not an easy topic to teach or write about. A lot of wonderful Christians are skeptical about "experiencing God's presence" because this topic has often been abused and distorted. You might hear about being "transformed by God's presence" and "hearing His voice" and think to yourself, "Keep all that weird stuff away from me!" I understand that completely, but if that's how you feel, let me tell you, this book is for you.

There's no replacement for real experience with God. You can be saved and know everything there is to know about Him, but until you experience His presence, your life will be incomplete.

Before I was even saved, I spent three years preaching, teaching and ministering. I knew the Bible and I knew about God, but I was missing the most important thing—I lacked my own true experience and relationship with God. I didn't actually know Him. That all changed in 1981. In a tiny motel room, God became real to me. He was no longer just someone I read about and preached about. I realized that I could know Him personally. As He filled the room and overwhelmed me with His presence, I gave my life to Him, and I've never been the same since.

Unfortunately, so many people live the way I lived before my life-changing encounter with God's presence. They know everything about God, but very few actually know Him. Too many people read the Bible, even teach the Bible, without actually having a personal relationship with the Lord.

Please hear me on this. I believe the Bible is critically important. It is the true, written word of God; but I also believe that you and I have the incredible opportunity to know the Author personally. We are meant to live and experience the Christian life, not just read about it. This can only happen when we know Him personally by spending time in His presence.

In this book, Alan reveals how every person can live in constant relationship with God. His conclusions are solid and biblical—I love that every point is clearly backed up by scripture. He also shares from personal experience. As you read Alan's stories of His encounters with God, I encourage you to believe that same relationship is available to you now.

The book you hold in your hands is so much more than a book ... it's an invitation to truly know God by walking in His presence daily. As you read Pastor Alan's wisdom, prepare to be transformed. When you experience God's presence, you will never, ever be the same again.

Robert Morris
Senior Pastor, Gateway Church
Bestselling author of *The Blessed Life*, *From Dream to Destiny*, and *The God I Never Knew*

1

What I Learned

Busted

"For I do not understand my own actions. For I do not do what I want, but I do the very thing I hate. Now if I do what I do not want, I agree with the law, that it is good." (Romans 7:15)

I was so busted.

I walked into the house Saturday night at eleven, and they were still up, waiting for me. Pastors Jack and Alta had been my teachers at a Bible college in Texas. I was living in their home, part of the small congregation they were pastoring in New England, trying to help some with weekend worship, and generally trying to figure out what to do with my life.

But I had a secret. There was stuff I was doing they didn't know about, or so I thought. That very night they had been praying together about the upcoming weekend services, and God let them in on my little secret. They knew stuff they had no way of knowing—I'm talking specifics here. I was so busted.

I was mortified and relieved at the same time; mortified because I had been exposed, relieved because keeping secrets was wearing me out. They weren't angry. I think they were sad. They were certainly very serious. Pastor Jack has a way of looking at you over the rims of his glasses and kind of cocking his head to one side when he is really getting down to business. I had been on the business end of this gaze before and recognized it immediately. It was intense, but these people loved me and I knew it. They didn't lecture or scold me, but they did draw some very clear boundaries and helped me begin a path to true freedom. They pastored me.

The thing is, I hated what I had been doing. At least part of me did. The part that didn't hate it—well, I didn't know how to control that guy. That's what I hated. The Paul I find in Romans 7:15 is my friend. I can relate to the struggle he describes so well. I'll bet I'm not the only one.

Twenty years later, I'm still on the path to freedom. I'm not the man I was, but I know He's not finished with me yet. I've been given the opportunity to help lots of people in their own pursuit of freedom as a pastor on staff at a great church. My contribution to this process is simply an overflow of what God has done and is doing in my own life.

Some of what I teach, I learned in classrooms and from books, but the stuff that really transformed me was more than just good information and helpful principles. In my life, where the rubber has met the road, what has truly changed me has been experiencing God's presence and voice—not merely learning and applying principles. This is what has shaped me from the inside out.

This book is my attempt to share what I've experienced, to give what I've received. It's not complete, because I'm not finished receiving. But there are some things I have begun to see. More than this, there are some new ways I'm learning to see that I'm convinced can help a lot of struggling, hurting people. I know because I was struggling, I was hurting—and I saw. I saw some new things, and I saw some old things in a new way.

Good Intentions

My life was all about good intentions. I intended to follow Jesus and represent Him well in every endeavor. I really did. When this didn't work, I intended to try harder. When that didn't work, I really intended to try harder. You get the idea.

I wasn't the only one with good intentions. I was raised in some good church environments where leaders really intended to make disciples. Their good intentions were clearly focused on helping me become a healthy and mature Christ follower. I really wanted to be a good disciple, and they really intended to help me become one. But there were some persistent, nagging patterns of thought, emotion, and behavior in me that remained unchanged despite all of our good intentions.

No matter how good your intentions, misunderstanding the problem will lead to wrong methods and solutions, ultimately leading to frustration and failure. Bob Hamp clarifies this so well when he says, "Often our solutions are as bad or worse than the problem we began with."[1] This is true because the solutions we choose to apply often serve only to reveal the ways we misunderstand the actual nature of our difficulties.

There are two discipleship models I've been exposed to in my church experiences. The first is an educational model that seeks to bring Christian maturity through the dissemination of Bible knowledge and doctrine. This model assumes my problem is ignorance and applies an educational solution to correct this problem. The difficulty here is that ignorance really is a problem. There's very little benefit to being ignorant or being a heretic, and there is therefore great value in strong biblical teaching and scriptural study. But what if ignorance is not really the root of my problem? If so, an educational discipleship model will prove insufficient.

The other primary discipleship approach is what I will call the legal model. Within this approach, the emphasis is not so much on knowing; it's on doing. Or not doing. There are varieties, of course! One version of the legal model focuses on prohibition—those things good Christians don't do. Various congregations and sects prohibit different kinds of things. My step-dad wasn't allowed to play cards in his church growing up. Some lists of forbidden behaviors are fairly standard: don't drink, don't smoke, don't cuss, don't chew; don't go out with girls

"But what if ignorance is not really the root of my problem?"

that do. Something like that, anyway. Some follow Jesus by prohibiting Harry Potter. Others seek to become like Christ by making girls wear ankle-length skirts. (I'm not sure if they're trying to help girls or boys become like Christ through this method. I suspect mostly boys.)

There is another common version of the legal model you might have been exposed to. The approach is prescriptive rather than prohibitive. The emphasis is on what you *should* do instead of what you shouldn't. You *should* read your Bible. You *should* pray. You *should* go to church.

The legal model, whether prohibitive or prescriptive, assumes my problem is behavioral. I do bad things; I need to do good things. This understanding of my problem brings me to the obvious solution: quit doing those bad things! Start doing good things. If this doesn't work, do the good things *harder!* [2]

A church REALLY committed to discipleship might adopt a comprehensive *one, two, three punch* approach to discipleship. This could involve a program of education for doctrinal instruction, along with a set of well-defined prohibited behaviors, plus a set of expectations for spiritual practices. All of these are implemented and enforced through a combination of formal congregational authority structures as well as through peer-driven social expectations.

Surely this would work, right? Well, it didn't work for me. Why? Is it wrong to identify and avoid destructive behaviors? Is it wrong to engage in healthy spiritual practices? Is it wrong to learn accurate doctrine from the Bible? Of course not. These things are good. They are simply insufficient, for they fail to accurately address the true extent of my problem. In those instances where genuine lasting transformation did occur within these discipleship models, something deeper was going on. Something more than information acquisition and rule following was happening.

What if we could identify and reproduce that?

Many of us who grew up in church had good intentions, but very few emerged into early adulthood in a way that accurately reflected Christ to the world. Trying harder didn't really seem to work. Why? We understood the human problem of sin in terms of ignorance and/or wrong behavior (and the resulting guilt from that behavior). What if these are only symptoms? What if there is a deeper underlying disease? Any combination of the educational and legal models of discipleship will prove less than effective simply because they only treat symptoms while the disease rages on.

If I believe that guilt is my root problem, then I will see forgiveness as my chief need, and I will understand and receive the provision of Jesus' sacrifice on the cross as God's way of removing my guilt. If ignorance is my root problem, then learning the Bible is my chief need, and I will understand and receive God's provision of scripture as God's chief educational tool.

But what if my problem is deeper than guilt? What if Adam and Eve's crime was much more than breaking a rule? What if God has provided for more than my forgiveness, followed by a return to good-intentioned rule following? What if my problem is deeper than ignorance? Our good intentions will not produce mature disciples if our solutions and methods are limited by a shallow understanding of the real problem.

What if no amount of accurate knowledge about God from the Bible will ever truly change me?

Finished

"When Jesus had received the sour wine, he said, "It is finished," and he bowed his head and gave up his spirit." (John 19:30)

It is finished. These three simple words say everything. My understanding of the human problem of sin may be limited, but I am sure God's is not. What Jesus accomplished on the cross has completely satisfied God. Provision has been fully made for lost humanity based on God's own comprehension of the nature of this problem. Hopefully, our own understanding of the problem will increase as we gain clarity from scripture regarding God's perspective. This new insight will enable us to more effectively and practically apply what God has provided for us through Christ. But nothing will change on God's end. He already understands the problem. He has already finished the solution. He has already provided what is needed. He has already given what was lacking, opened what was closed, and restored what was lost.

Stepping into deeper levels of true freedom is simply a result of appropriating the finished work of Christ on the cross. Freedom cannot be attained any other way.

It is finished. We may need to see differently. We may need to receive more deeply. We may need to respond in new ways. But if there is any transforming effect to any of this, it will not be because God has added something to Jesus' finished work. If there is any way forward for us, it will be in drinking more deeply from the river of living water to which He has already given us access. If transformation into the image of Christ is really possible, it will be because we have more fully surrendered to the grace already given. It is finished. Jesus died, rose on the third day, and is exalted to God's right hand. There is no other victory for us than this.

> *"He has already finished the solution. He has already provided what is needed. He has already given what was lacking, opened what was closed, and restored what was lost."*

Take Off Your Shoes

Not too long ago, I spent a week with a group of men on a 500-acre ranch in the Texas Hill Country. While some of this time was devoted to praying, sharing, and worshipping together, much of it was spent alone with God out in nature.

I left the lodge at 8:00 am with my walking stick, backpack and a camping chair in tow. In my backpack I carried my Bible, journal, pen, insect repellent, sunscreen, bottled water, pocketknife, and a pair of clean socks.

It was a beautiful day, warm and sunny. There were a few white puffs of cloud scurrying here and there about the sky. I wandered for a while through fields, over fences, and past the less-than-curious stares of a few cows and horses. It was very quiet. The only sounds were an occasional breeze and the songs of a bird or two. Finally, I came to a place where the river wound through a ravine. On my side, the path moved gradually down to the river's edge. On the opposite bank, a cliff swept steeply up toward the sky where a couple of buzzards could be seen circling and waiting for calamity to strike some unsuspecting creature.

I found a nice spot, set up my camping chair, and applied a good amount of sunscreen to my fair city-boy skin. I took a sip of water, and sat down to read, pray, and journal. I had eight hours to fill, so I was concerned when it only took me about half an hour to complete my assigned reading and response for the morning.

With no particular agenda, I asked, "Lord, anything You want to talk about?"

Let's talk about your parents' divorce.

Gulp.

I grabbed my journal and a pen, prepared to scribble down any forthcoming insights about this significant moment from my childhood.

Take off your shoes and wade out into the river.

Huh?

Silence.

Not my usual *quiet time* methodology, but ok. I unlaced my hiking boots, peeled off my socks (already somewhat unpleasant), rolled up my knee length shorts as high as possible, and waded in. The water was clear and cold, the current slow. I remember the gentle steady rippling sound of the water moving by. Some small and a few medium sized fish darted this way and that. The smaller ones usually hung out in groups, while the bigger ones wandered more confidently alone. At the more shallow points, the water reached my knees; at deeper points, my mid-thigh; and at the deepest points, my shorts, which were rolled up high enough to make Larry Bird proud; but keeping them dry was futile nevertheless.

I don't know how long I stayed out there, wandering slowly back and forth in the middle of the channel. I suppose I covered about a hundred-yard stretch multiple times. It lasted maybe an hour and a half.

God met with me in that river.

We talked about my parents' divorce, an event I don't even remember because I was only three years old at the time. He told me things I already knew but needed to hear Him say; though until I heard them, I didn't know I needed them. He told me things I didn't know, and clarified some things about which I was misinformed. I cried a bit, but not as much as I might have expected. I asked questions. He answered some, but not all of them. He asked me questions, too—questions that work like a surgeon's scalpel, questions that bring light into darkness, questions that cut away cancer in the soul. He's not long-winded. He uses small words and short phrases that deliver power and peace with a transforming strength that washes, and frees, and heals.

I knew when this was done. Don't ask me how, but I knew.

"I feel like I should dip all the way into the water."

If I've washed your feet, all of you is clean.

Now I wept.

As I stepped out of the river, I felt less afraid. I didn't know it was fear until it wasn't there anymore. We didn't really talk about fear. We had talked about love, and now I felt safe.

I thought about putting on my clean socks, but decided to put the others back on again. Better save the clean ones in case I really need them.

Let's Stand and Sing Together

I've taken a lot of classes through the years, few better than one I took many years ago called *Deliverance*. I signed up for it based on the title. I wasn't sure what deliverance was, but I was quite certain I needed it. The instructor was a man named Dutch Sheets. You may have heard of him; he has since written some very helpful books and I recommend them highly.

It was a twelve-week class. Some classes are so dull and tedious any excuse to skip will do, but not this class. Mr. Sheets is a gifted Bible teacher, and it always felt like something more was happening in the room than could be written down in a notebook. But the notebook stuff was fantastic too. He saw things in scripture I'd never noticed, and he seemed to see them in a different way, a way I didn't have words for but longed to see as well.

About five minutes before each class, he would begin writing on the dry-erase board as the students filed in and milled about looking for a seat, visiting with each other. There were about four hundred of us, so this was quite a noisy few minutes. He would write various things— Greek words, Hebrew words (using English letters; none of us know how to read Greek or Hebrew), and English terms—things he intended to cover during the lecture, which we would want to capture in our notebooks.

I never missed one of these classes. I was learning things I knew I needed to learn academically, but more was happening. Something in my heart felt like it was stirring. It seemed like waking up from a sleep. It felt like being blind but beginning to see, with eyes I'd never used before.[3] I couldn't put words to it at the time; I just didn't miss any classes.

One particular day, about eight classes in, I arrived as

usual, found my seat, and began to copy the contents of the dry-erase board. Suddenly, I felt something very deep and very strong.

Anticipation.

It felt like that moment on a roller coaster when you reach the top of the hill

"It felt like being blind but beginning to see, with eyes I'd never used before."

just prior to free falling and everything freezes for a moment too short to count. I froze. Mr. Sheets froze too. His marker went still and he, for the briefest moment, was like a statue. The whole room was instantly quiet, a remarkable thing in itself. Everyone seemed suddenly aware of the same strong sense of anticipation I was feeling. Our teacher very gently and very intentionally set his marker down, turned on his heel, and walked slowly and deliberately to the edge of the platform.

"Let's stand and sing together."

"Father, we love You. We praise You. We adore You. Glorify Thy name in all the earth."

We never reached the *in all the earth* part.

God came. It was sudden. It was unexpected. We hit the deck, four hundred of us on our faces. It was in one sense like being knocked down. But it also felt like falling, because I lost my capacity to stand. But it also felt like choosing to get as low as possible before something or Someone very high. But it also felt like a weight pressing me to the floor. I don't think I could have stood up if I tried, but attempting it did not even occur to me. It's hard to describe.

Before my nose hit the carpet, I began to weep. So did everyone else, as I recall, and it wasn't a nice cry. It was a moan, a wail. It rose from deep down, with a pressure behind it that erupted with volume and violence. It went on for an hour at least. It was wonderful, and awful.

When I finally got up, I was spent, exhausted—and changed.

I learned things in that class. Some of them made it to my notebook.

What I Learned

I've had lots of these experiences over the years; some quite dramatic, many much less so. I wish I had more than I have, but I'm thankful for these stories. They keep coming and this makes me happy. What I've learned from all this, what I'm still learning, is the kind of transformation I need doesn't come from education or behavior modification. The kind of transformation I need comes from experiencing God's presence and voice.

I hope this doesn't scare you. It has scared many before, who would much rather avoid things beyond their control. They're much more comfortable in the safer realms of classrooms and religious social mores than in the stretching places of experiential spirituality. But there really is no other method of transformation. God has offered us Himself. He has made a way for us to know Him experientially and relationally, and this is what transforms humans into Christ's image; there is no back-up plan.

I've learned that learning is insufficient. I've learned that trying harder is futile. I've learned that spiritual disciplines and right doctrine produce wonderful Pharisees but do not heal the broken. I've learned that the good news the gospel offers is better than I ever imagined.

2

Avoiding God

A Kingdom of Priests

"Now therefore, if you will indeed obey my voice and keep my covenant, you shall be my treasured possession among all peoples, for all the earth is mine; and you shall be to me a kingdom of priests and a holy nation. These are the words that you shall speak to the people of Israel." (Exodus 19:5–6)

Experiential spirituality can be uncomfortable. In Exodus 19, God expressed His heart to Moses. He wanted everyone to experience His presence and hear His voice, to be a *kingdom of priests*. Though there were different roles and certain parameters for the whole experience, no one was to be excluded. They were all given three days' notice to prepare. No sex. Don't touch the mountain. Take a bath. God is coming.

And come He did. It was dramatic to say the least:

"Now when all the people saw the thunder and the flashes of lightning and the sound of the trumpet and the mountain smoking, the people were afraid and trembled, and they stood far off and said to Moses, 'You speak to us, and we will listen; but do not let God speak to us, lest we die.' Moses said to the people, 'Do not fear, for God has come to test you, that the fear of him may be before you, that you may not sin.' The people stood far off, while Moses drew near to the thick darkness where God was." (Exodus 20:18–21)

This whole *personal relationship with God* thing that sounded so good as a concept is a bit troublesome as a reality. Wide-eyed, a bit shaky, and some distance around the clock from thinking of any kind of dinner plans, the collective discussion begins.

"That was ... something, wasn't it?"

"Yeah. Sure was."

"Not sure I could handle a regular dose of that."

"Whew. Thought I was the only one who felt that way. What a relief!"

"Well, somebody needs to tell Moses we are more

comfortable with a less experiential brand of religion." I've heard similar discussions in church. Haven't you? We don't mind if there are a select few, like Moses or Aaron, or maybe your senior pastor, or maybe your favorite televangelist who seek God themselves, who experience God, who actually have encounters with Him. We just don't want that ourselves. Let Moses come down off the mountain and tell us about God. Tell us what He said. Give us the information. Give us the doctrine. Give us the principles. You go near. We'll stand at a distance.

But this wasn't God's desire. He wanted everyone to encounter Him. He wanted a kingdom of priests (see Exodus 19:5-6 above). If this is true in the Old Covenant, how much more in the New? God's heart has always been for His people to really know Him, but we have historically been more at ease with words written on tablets of stone or in a book. Knowing about God is fine. Knowing Him—now that's scary, and we often avoid it.

Missing the Point

There's nothing wrong with the book He has given us. Scripture is a wonderful and essential part of our experience with God. For one thing, it's full of stories about people who experienced God themselves. It helps us see the story of Creation, Redemption, and New Creation from a thirty-thousand foot perspective.[1] In the Bible we see clearly what only God can do, the thing we could never do ourselves. We also see the things expected of us, those things God will not do for us. Scripture provides guardrails for our own experience of God, ensuring that our relationship makes sense within the bigger picture of what God is up to, keeping us from deception and error.

I love studying scripture. As the years go by, I find myself increasingly convinced of the inspiration and authority of the Bible—and I didn't begin as a skeptic. But it's not hard to miss the point of scripture. Many did in Jesus' day and many still do. I know I've missed the point myself more times than I care to recall. I've even taught others to do the same.

There's a key passage of scripture that lays this out for us better than anything else I know. I want you to slow down, and read it carefully. Reflect on the significance of what Jesus is saying here to some very sincere religious people.

"And the Father who sent me has himself borne witness about me. His voice you have never heard, his form you have never seen, and you do not have his word abiding in you, for you do not believe the one whom he has sent. You search the Scriptures because you think that in them you have eternal life; and it is they that bear witness about me, yet you refuse to come to me that you may have life." (John 5:37–40)

We must first notice that the group of people Jesus is addressing *search the Scriptures.* These are not passive readers of scripture, content with a daily Bible verse and a few devotional thoughts. Through intense inquiry and exploration, they are seeking insight and understanding. Jesus is speaking here to serious students of scripture. As

"..it's not hard to miss the point of scripture."

admirable and positive as this surely seems to us, Jesus' tone is not positive.

Look what He says to them: *His voice you have never heard, his form you have never seen.* Jesus is reprimanding this group of Bible students. For what? For a lack of experience. They know scripture, but they've never heard God's voice. They've missed the point. He then clarifies they don't *have his word abiding* in them.

There's something more available in and through scripture than what they have gained. There's evidently something about this *word* that can abide within, take up residence inside. Sound a bit mystical? Definitely. But there it is. They have completely given themselves to the book and yet somehow missed out on the author of the book, thereby missing out on the primary purpose of the book.

Why would anyone make this mistake? They have come to embrace a serious misconception about the nature of the book. Why have they invested their lives in the exploration of it? What is their fundamental assumption and motive? Jesus gives the answer in verse 40: *Because you think that in them [the scriptures] you have eternal life.*

Uncomfortable with standing near the mountain, God's people have elected to stand far off and let Moses approach God. Fearful of knowing the author of the book, they have become satisfied with His book alone, even going so far as to think of the book as being their source of eternal life. Jesus acknowledges that the book accurately tells them about Him, and then He points out the thing they haven't done yet.

> "*It is they that bear witness about me, **yet you refuse to come to me that you may have life.**" (John 5:40b emphasis added)

What haven't they done? What have they refused to do? They've refused to come to Him. Where does life come from? Not from the book, but from the author of the book—the one the book points us toward.

The implications of these verses are stunning. Apparently, it's possible to intently explore the scripture and never know the Word, never hear His voice, never experience His presence. When this is true about us, we've missed the point entirely, and no amount of study will fix us.

Remove encounter between God and man from the Bible, and what are we left with? Mainly, we are left with doctrine and morals—the accurate information about God we need to learn and affirm, and the right behaviors we need to conform to. We end up with the two discipleship models prevalent in the church today: the educational model and the legal model.

This pharisaic approach to scripture excludes *knowing* God in the name of knowing *about* God. One kind of knowing is merely conceptual, the way I know about dinosaurs. The other kind of knowing is intimate, relational, and experiential, the way I know my wife. Merely knowing *about* God excludes relating to Him in the name of obeying Him. It demands much from us, but does little to empower us to do any of it well. We learn, but we do not know. We follow rules, but never truly surrender. We conform, but we are not transformed.

The Contemporary Appeal

It's no wonder this educational and legal approach to faith has gained such traction in our day. Western culture since the Enlightenment has become increasingly hostile to spiritual experience. Reason has become the only legitimate way of knowing and the five senses are the only endorsed source of data, especially if this data can be reproduced in a lab. Science has labored hard to define for us any possible origin other than a Creator. Spiritual experience is unpopular at best, and outright rejected in most cases. Francis Schaeffer makes this point with great clarity.

> ... *The consensus upon which our culture was built has shifted from one that was largely Christian (though we must say immediately it was far from perfect) to a consensus growing out of the Enlightenment: that is, to a consensus that stands in total antithesis to Christian truth at every point—including the denial of the supernatural; belief in the all-sufficiency of human reason; the rejection of the fall; denial of the deity of Christ and his resurrection; belief in the perfectibility of Man; and the destruction of the Bible.* [2]

Walk up to a coworker tomorrow and announce God spoke to you in a dream during the night and watch how he responds. But this would be a very biblically based spiritual experience, wouldn't it? Relate a personal experience of God's miraculous power and many, even those in our churches, will have an immediate gut reaction that states, *There has to be a natural explanation for that!*

It is imperative we better understand this phenomenon, as it is deeply imbedded in the way we tend to see things.

It's the filter through which we experience life, our lenses. For those who desire to not merely know about God, but to truly know Him, this perspective on reality must be adjusted in significant ways. We need a new prescription for our lenses.

My family likes to visit a large amusement park in our community. It's big enough that it is sometimes necessary to look at a map of the park in order to get where you want to go. The most important feature of the map is the big red arrow next to the caption that reads, *You are here.* Knowing where you are now is the first step toward getting where you're going. The same is true in our case. If our goal is to see reality through a biblical set of lenses, we first need to better understand the ones we've got.

"We need a new prescription for our lenses."

If we believe in God at all here in the West, we tend to think of Him as being far away and uninvolved in our affairs. He's like an expert watchmaker who designs, builds, and winds the watch, but then His part is done. The watch runs without His intervention by the rules He designed. We see reality as a closed system that operates by natural laws, by cause and effect.[3] This view, if it includes God at all, affirms His transcendence but denies His immanence. In other words, it allows God to be *other* than creation and even *over* all creation, but it will not allow Him to be near and involved, moment by moment, *within* creation.

Liberal theologians are those who apply this view of things to scripture itself and deny the supernatural in the Bible. Many conservative theologians are those who affirm the supernatural in the Bible, but claim He doesn't do that sort of thing anymore in an era where it would be so out of style.

This more conservative view allows well-intentioned Christ followers to hang on to the authority and inspiration of scripture—not denying the supernatural content—without having to maintain any expectation in the present for direct experience with God. This set of lenses is very popular and exceptionally useful, for it allows scripture to maintain authority about doctrine and morality without infringing on our naturalistic, materialistic, non-biblical worldview. It keeps God at a distance where we can manage Him without difficulty. This is not a new motive. Go back and read Exodus 19-20 again.

Eastern Encroachment

In the Eastern part of our small planet, a different view prevails, and it's really the polar opposite of our Western view. There, god is seen as being present and involved moment by moment within our world, but NOT as being *other* than us and certainly NOT *over* us.[4] He is immanent, but not transcendent. God is near because everything is god. You are god. I'm god. The trees are god. The dolphins are god. Everything is one. There is no creator/creation distinction.

This view of things is gaining popularity in our hemisphere, because there is something deep within us longing for spiritual experience. The secular Western view offers none. And the church offers little help, conformed as it is to this secular view, denying any present expectation of spiritual experience with God. So the only avenue of spiritual pursuit lies in Eastern spirituality or some contemporary New Age adaptation, all with the side benefit of not having to ultimately answer to a God who is both *other* than us and *over* us. Bonus. Spirituality without accountability can be quite appealing if you're looking for that sort of thing.

Biblical Expectation

Scripture demands an expectation of spiritual experience, of divine encounter. Any version of the Faith that minimizes this expectation is incongruent with scripture itself.

"Having the appearance of godliness, but denying its power. Avoid such people." (2 Timothy 3:5)

The Greek word translated *power* in this verse is

dunamis, the very same word used to describe Jesus' miraculous power. Much of my experience within churches has made excellent sense of this verse for me. When we deny the power of God, we are left merely with a form of godliness—form with little or no substance.

As one who knows what it is to hear and proclaim a powerless gospel, few passages of scripture challenge me more than this one from the end of Paul's letter to the Romans. As Paul is wrapping up this doctrinal show of force, look how he himself defines what it means to fully proclaim the good news:

> *"In Christ Jesus, then, I have reason to be proud of my work for God. For I will not venture to speak of anything except what Christ has accomplished through me to bring the Gentiles to obedience—by **word and deed**, by the power of **signs and wonders**, by the **power of the Spirit** of God—so that from Jerusalem and all the way around to Illyricum I have **fulfilled the ministry of the gospel** of Christ; and thus I make it my ambition to preach the gospel, not where Christ has already been named, lest I build on someone else's foundation,"* (Romans 15:17–20 emphasis added)

The New King James Version translates it this way: *I have fully preached the gospel of Christ.*

The full proclamation of the gospel, according to Paul,

is not just in word but also in deed. And lest we assume he's talking about some kind of social welfare program, he then says, *by the power of signs and wonders, by the power of the Spirit of God.*

The strong implication of this passage is that the full proclamation of the gospel of Jesus contains an expectation of the demonstration of God's power.[5] Spiritual experience is deeply imbedded in the gospel itself. The very birth of the Church strongly reinforces this expectation.

Perhaps you are familiar with the story of Pentecost in Acts 2. Jesus has ascended into heaven, leaving clear instruction that His followers are to stay in Jerusalem and wait for the promise of the Holy Spirit. After ten days of waiting in an upper room, about 120 followers have a dramatic encounter with God, creating such a scene that 3,000 men plus women and children end up converting to faith in Christ in a single day.

Peter, in his impromptu sermon on that occasion, explains their experience as the fulfillment of God's promise from the prophet Joel.

"And it shall come to pass afterward, that I will pour out my Spirit on all flesh; your sons and your daughters shall prophesy, your old men shall dream dreams, and your young men shall see visions. Even on the male and female servants in those days I will pour out

my Spirit." (Joel 2:28–29)

Lest we assume this kind of encounter was reserved for a select few at a select time, He says this is intended for *all flesh*. It is for males and females. It is for the young and the old; it is even for servants and slaves.

It's for everyone.

How does Peter conclude?

"And Peter said to them, 'Repent and be baptized every one of you in the name of Jesus Christ for the forgiveness of your sins, and you will receive the gift of the Holy Spirit. For the promise is for you and for your children and for all who are far off, everyone whom the Lord our God calls to himself." (Acts 2:38–39)

Who is this promise for?

It is for everyone.

God calls everyone to Himself, regardless of time or geography. Jesus' own expectation articulated in Mark's account of the Great Commission provides powerful insight.

"And he said to them, 'Go into all the world and proclaim the gospel to the whole creation. Whoever believes and is baptized will be saved, but whoever does not believe will be condemned. And these signs

will accompany those who believe: in my name they
will cast out demons; they will speak in new tongues;
they will pick up serpents with their hands; and if
they drink any deadly poison, it will not hurt them;
they will lay their hands on the sick, and they will
recover." (Mark 16:15–18)

The geographic context is *all the world.* This is where the gospel is to be proclaimed. What will be the results in all the world? Some will believe. Others won't. No surprises here.

But look at what He says next. Those who believe are going to be in for quite a ride, aren't they? Note here it doesn't just say those who are proclaiming the gospel will do these things. Those who respond to the message with faith will also be doing these things. Where? In all the world. There is absolutely no biblical expectation of a gospel without power, of a religion without spiritual experience, of doctrine and morals without divine encounter.

Changing Lenses

So what do we do?

How do I trade in my post-Enlightenment, Western, secular, naturalistic, materialistic set of lenses for some biblical ones? The answer is not as easy as you might think.

Many churches theologically affirm God's presence and power, but demonstrate neither. Your first thought might be to study more and simply correct your doctrine about such things. But this can't possibly be the solution because it is *in fact* the problem. I've laid out a decent scriptural argument for a present expectation of spiritual experience; you might even agree with me. But what is to prevent this from being simply one more doctrine we affirm?

How did we really get these lenses to begin with? There are many factors, some of which I've already addressed; but the main issue is experience.

We tend to believe what we've experienced and deny what we haven't. It's as simple as that. Most of the Western church at large has never seen a 'live demonstration' of the kind of power we read about in the Word, and much of contemporary theology reflects this lack of experience. This creates a dynamic tension between the experience of powerlessness and scripture's clear promise of power. This tension is resolved by developing theologies which remove the expectation of God's power in the present era, relegating expressions of God's power to either Bible times or the future Kingdom. These new theological explanations diminish any expectation of God's power in the present and thereby perpetuate the lack of experience.

All I've given you in this chapter is an argument. The very problem I'm describing informs me this argument alone will do little or nothing to change your expectation. But experience might.

3

The Importance of Hearing

"For all who are led by the Spirit of God are sons of God."
(Romans 8:14)

Led By the Spirit

The phone rang, jarring me out of my Excel spreadsheet-induced trance.

"Alan Smith, Financial Controls. How can I help you?"

"Alan, how in the world did you see our post so quickly?"

I was working as a contractor for a large telecom company; managing statements of work in the financial controls division of their data services section. Sounds exciting, I know. I'd been there for a while and was genuinely grateful for the job and the paycheck, but I can't say

I was really enjoying it.

What I wanted to do with my time and energy was vocational ministry. I'd spent most of my twenties in ministry, but a failed church plant attempt ejected me rather harshly from that field and all efforts toward re-entry had been futile. God seems very comfortable with allowing life circumstances to squeeze us uncomfortably. I was being squeezed. Big time.

One year prior, I had decided that since ministry wasn't presently a realistic option, what I really wanted to try was sales. I wasn't interested in just any sales position. My friend Tom owned a mid-sized company, and I really wanted to work for him. For me, it was more about an opportunity to be mentored by him than anything else. There was an opening for a regional sales manager, and I applied. I was completely unqualified for the position, as my résumé demonstrated in great detail. I had no relevant education, no relevant sales experience, and no relevant industry experience. All I had was a personal connection to Tom; that at least got me an interview with the national sales manager, who didn't know me at all.

"Asking puts me in a position of humility, dependence, and expectation."

I wasn't scared, though; I was quite confident, because

while praying about the opportunity, I felt I had heard God tell me I was going to get the job.

Now I must pause at this point and offer some description of what it's like for me when I hear God's voice. Some of you may have little to no frame of reference for such things and, therefore, no way to even begin recognizing such experiences if they were ever to happen to you. I've been there; the point of this book is to help with exactly this sort of thing.

I experience God's voice primarily as thoughts that enter my mind. At times they come as short words and phrases, other times as images or mental pictures, and sometimes just impressions, sort of like inward nudges.

Occasionally these experiences are unlooked for, but usually, for me, they come in response to questions I ask God. It seems like there's something about asking God questions that positions me to hear and receive. *Asking* puts me in a position of humility, dependence, and expectation.

The words, phrases, images, and impressions don't seem to come linearly or in any sort of progression. When you're listening to a friend speak, their words come to your head through your ears one word at a time. Your brain is then able to translate this linear progression of symbols into a single thought or idea. That's not how it seems to work between God and me; it's actually quite the opposite. God's words, phrases, images, and impressions sort of emerge into my consciousness fully formed. Then my brain has to unpack them into a linear sequence of words if I have any intention of writing them down or speaking them out loud to someone else. The receiving is intuitive, not analytical.

This is not without parallel in my relational experience. I've been married to Nancy for seventeen years and we can communicate this way. She can elbow me under the table at a dinner party when needed and through this communication, this *impression* comes to me fully formed; my brain has learned to immediately unpack this revelation into a linear sequence of words I can clearly understand. *Quit talking, Alan. You are nearing the 'inappropriate border' in this story. I know it's funny, but you need to quit while you're ahead.* She didn't say these things, but she did communicate them with great clarity.

So, when I say I felt like God told me I was going to get the job, that's what I mean. I asked God for the job, and I immediately got the impression He said *Yes.* I'm not really sure if this was just a sense my brain translated into words, or if the words themselves came along with the impression. But this is the way I've experienced God's voice, and it has happened enough times that I've grown comfortable with the process.

Thus, I was quite confident during the interview process—a very long and tedious interview process dragging out for several months. There were one-on-one meetings.

There were panel interviews. There were several other candidates. There were weeks where I heard nothing. I hate being in limbo, so I found this to be very frustrating at times.

Finally, it came down to me and one other candidate, a man with vast sales experience within this particular industry. But was I worried? Absolutely not. I had heard God. Faith comes by hearing (see Romans 10:17). It was a lock.

The call informing me they were offering the position to the other candidate came as quite a shock. I was disappointed because of the rejection, because I wouldn't be changing jobs, wouldn't receive an increase in compensation, wouldn't get a chance to be mentored by Tom; but most of all, I was devastated because I had missed it. I just knew I had heard God, and clearly, I hadn't. Of course I had missed it before (remember the failed church plant), but this one hit me especially hard.

I hunkered down and kept going to work every day wrestling spreadsheets at the telecom company.

One year later, I was at my desk in my little cubicle. My keyboard was steaming from all the great spreadsheet work I was doing. My desk was stacked with folders and documents in various stages of approval and confirmation. Emails were coming in as if from a rapid-fire machine gun. The phone was ringing. Good times, man. Good times.

All of a sudden, I had one of those moments where God's voice bursts in unexpectedly. Without warning, the phrase *Send Tom your résumé right now* jumped out from around the corner and stood there inside my head with vivid clarity.

So I did. What did I have to lose, right? I already didn't have the job. I pulled up the file from my computer, dusted it off a bit, and attached it to an email addressed to Tom and his VP of Human Resources, Linda.

Five minutes later …

The phone rang, jarring me out of my Excel spreadsheet-induced trance.

"Alan Smith, Financial Controls. How can I help you?"

"Alan, how in the world did you see our post so quickly?" It was Linda.

"What post?"

"Five minutes ago, I clicked *submit* on Monster, reposting the very same position you applied for last year. Not five seconds later, I received an email with your résumé. This is kind of freaking me out."

"Me too, Linda." Me too.

> *"What we have or haven't experienced sets the bar for what we do and don't expect from God."*

I got the job.

Is This Weird?

Is this weird? That's a terrific question. I'm sure it seems quite weird to some of you. And by *weird*, I mean *outside the norm*. Does God still operate that way? Is it realistic for me to expect God to work in my life this way? Who gets to define *the norm?*

For most of us church folks, the norm has been defined by what we have or haven't experienced up to this point. Another way of saying this is we've allowed our experience to define *normal*. What we experience determines what is normal; what we consider to be normal is authoritative, and thus our experience becomes our authority. What we have or haven't experienced sets the bar for what we do and don't expect from God.

Wait. I thought scripture was supposed to be the authority in my life? But for many, it isn't. Our experiences authoritatively shape our expectations and become obstacles obstructing our ability to allow the Bible to define what is the norm. Experience defines our theology. This is a dangerous path indeed, and one well travelled in our time.

Sons of God

I began this chapter with a power-packed little verse of scripture from Paul's letter to the Romans.

"For all who are led by the Spirit of God are sons of God." (Romans 8:14)

This sounds very nice. It's short, but full of lots of great Bible words like *Spirit* and *God* and even *sons of God*. Romans is Paul's doctrinal tour de force. This verse is inspired, and therefore authoritative. What if we were to dig deeper, specifically to allow this verse to define our norm?

The important category Paul is defining is *sons of God*. It includes everyone who believes in Jesus and is therefore quite comprehensive.

"But to all who did receive him, who believed in his name, he gave the right to become children of God." (John 1:12)

In Romans 8:14, Paul is giving us a key characteristic, marking those who are sons of God. Namely, that they are *led by the Spirit*. The following verses give us some insight into this concept. The Spirit *bears witness with our spirit*; this means the Spirit speaks to us. What He speaks to us about is our identity as God's children and the inheritance that goes along with that: who we are, whose we are, and what belongs to us as a result. I believe all of this is packed up within Paul's meaning when he uses the phrase *led by the Spirit*.

The word *led* directly speaks to the idea of influence and guidance. So, what is the biblical norm for God's children? We should expect God, by His Spirit, to influence, guide, and direct our lives in a manner that includes Him speaking to us.

However, it's always dangerous to build a doctrine, or establish a norm, based on a single verse. So the next question for us ought to be: are there any scriptural instances of this understanding of Romans 8:14 being lived out by those in relationship with God? Does God, in the Bible, influence, guide, and direct the lives of His followers by speaking to them through His Spirit?

I would challenge you to find very many places in the Bible where this *doesn't* happen. Read the Old Testament stories. Read about the life of Jesus Himself in the gospels. Read the book of Acts! This expectation, this norm, is not some marginal idea shoved into a corner—it's a major biblical theme. God wants to talk to us. He wants to guide and direct our lives, and invites us into this kind of living day by day.

"To him the gatekeeper opens. The sheep hear his voice, and he calls his own sheep by name and leads them out. When he has brought out all his own, he goes before them, and the sheep follow him, for they know his voice. A stranger they will not follow, but they will flee from him, for they do not know the voice

of strangers." (John 10:3–5)

How Important is This?

Saying *yes* to one thing means saying *no,* or at least *not yet,* to others. Prioritization is a fact of life. The Bible challenges us in many ways, and it is difficult to consider responding to all of them at once. Loving your neighbor, for instance, might take precedence over women praying with their heads covered in church. Both are in the Bible, and at some point both need to be taken seriously; but if you have to say *yes* to one of these, don't be rude to your neighbor because you're locked in trying to interpret Paul's thoughts on head coverings.

Likewise, we need to consider the issue of priority when exploring what the Bible presents as a norm regarding hearing God's voice and being led by the Spirit. How important is this? Take a look at the following verse:

"So faith comes from hearing, and hearing through the word of Christ." (Romans 10:17)

How important is hearing God in the life of a believer? Let's answer that with another question: how important is faith in the life of a believer? Let's follow that with another question: is it even possible to become a believer without faith? Faith is what produces believers. Hearing God speak is what produces faith. So hearing God and being led by the Spirit is of the utmost priority, and its importance cannot be overstated.

Now don't misread this verse. Romans 10:17 is not saying faith comes from reading the Bible. Reading the Bible is great, but plenty of people do that and don't experience faith as a result. This verse is overtly stating faith comes from hearing Jesus speak to me. Of course, one of the primary ways Jesus speaks to me is through scripture, but John 5:37-40, which we looked at earlier, makes it clear it is very possible to search scripture and never hear God speak. The Bible is loaded with stories of God speaking directly to His people, by His Spirit. This is what produces faith!

"Faith is ultimately my response to God's grace."

Faith, rather than being something I initiate, is ultimately my response to God's grace. He speaks and I respond with trust. He calls and I answer. In trusting Him, I draw near, and this is what pleases Him.

"And without faith it is impossible to please him, for whoever would draw near to God must believe that he exists and that he rewards those who seek him." (Hebrews 11:6)

How important is hearing God? It is clearly a biblical norm of the highest priority in the life of every believer. Any discipleship that excludes teaching people how to hear and respond to the voice of God is no discipleship at all, for without hearing God there is no faith. Without faith, there is no Christian life.

Notice in Hebrews 11:6, the very definition of faith involves drawing near to God with the expectation of His response. Faith that is pleasing to God results in spiritual experience, divine encounter.

Is Hearing God only for the Mature in Christ?

At this point, some will agree that hearing God is certainly very important, but perhaps something we should expect only from the mature believer. But what if this kind of experience is something we can realistically expect from every believer, regardless of maturity? Let's take a look at some familiar verses from earlier in Romans 10.

> "*Because, if you confess with your mouth that Jesus is Lord and believe in your heart that God raised him from the dead, you will be saved. For with the heart one believes and is justified, and with the mouth one confesses and is saved.*" (Romans 10:9–10)

As we saw in Romans 10:17, faith comes from hearing

Jesus speak; this passage is about brand new believers! Faith resulting from hearing Christ speak is not merely for the mature; it is the very entry point of our life in Christ. This becomes clear when we add verse eight:

> *"But what does it say? "The word is near you, in your mouth and in your heart" (that is, the word of faith that we proclaim); because, if you confess with your mouth that Jesus is Lord and believe in your heart that God raised him from the dead, you will be saved. For with the heart one believes and is justified, and with the mouth one confesses and is saved."* (Romans 10:8–10)

What precedes the faith and confession that appropriate salvation in a person's life? The word comes near. We hear the voice of God speaking to us even in the presentation of the gospel; faith can come no other way. No one can experience the salvation Jesus has provided apart from hearing the voice of God. Think of your own conversion experience. What, in addition to the mere transmission of data, was going on inside you? What were you sensing? How was the Holy Spirit tugging on your heart? If you can put into words what that was like, then you already have a point of reference for what it's like for you to hear God's voice.

Hearing God is for every believer, new and mature.

There's no other way to become one. Hearing God in the *presentation* of the gospel is distinct from merely hearing the gospel, for many hear the gospel and don't believe.

Once someone has heard Christ in this way and responded with faith and confession, they are saved. It is at this point the two primary discipleship models we have discussed previously are usually brought into view.

It tends to go something like this:

Now that you are a believer, we have a class we want you to attend (the educational model). In this class, we want you to understand there are some behaviors you should, as a believer, not be involved in (prohibitive legal model). Additionally, as a believer, you should pray, read your Bible, attend church, etc. (This is the prescriptive legal model.) Those who began their walk with Christ by responding to the living voice of His Spirit are now continuing their walk by the methods of doctrinal instruction and rule keeping.

Paul wrote the letter to the Galatians to address this exact issue. Believers converted through spiritual experience and divine encounter had been tricked into attempting spiritual growth by another means.

"O foolish Galatians! Who has bewitched you? It was before your eyes that Jesus Christ was publicly portrayed as crucified. Let me ask you only this: Did you receive the Spirit by works of the law or by hear-

ing with faith? Are you so foolish? Having begun by the Spirit, are you now being perfected by the flesh?" (Galatians 3:1–3)

Paul is not simply contrasting faith with law; he's being much more pointed and specific than that. He is contrasting *the hearing of faith* and receiving *the Spirit* with *the works of the law* and *the flesh*. It is not just faith; it is the hearing of faith. Paul's entire argument is that the way you begin is the way you should continue. The way you enter is the way you are perfected. Hearing Jesus speak to you, being led by the Spirit, is what makes you a son of God. It is also what brings you into maturity. There are no mature believers who don't know how to hear God's voice, and there are no immature believers who can't hear God; it is impossible to be a believer any other way.

What I Really Learned

When I finally got the job working for Tom, what did I really receive? A job? A paycheck? A great opportunity to grow and develop under the influence of a wonderful mentor? Yes, but I received more. I learned more. I'm not talking about the kind of learning that informs; I'm talking about the kind of learning that brings understanding, shapes the lenses through which we perceive reality, and forms our core beliefs about God, ourselves, and the nature of reality.

I learned God speaks to me, and I can hear Him. I learned God is near, and intimately involved in the affairs of my life. I learned God is good, and works in my life to do good in and through me. I learned God is powerful and able to arrange and orchestrate very complex details and events in order to accomplish His purpose. I learned He must think I am quite valuable in order to go to this kind of trouble. I learned that sometimes, when circumstances tell me I can't hear God or I've somehow blown it, I shouldn't be too quick to judge.

I learned lots of things, some of them important beyond quantifying, simply because God told me what job to apply for, that I would get the job, and when to send my résumé and to whom. I heard. I responded. This is the life of faith, and it is available to you. You can't learn these kinds of things by reading this paragraph; unless, of course, you are listening not just to me, but to Him.

4

My Heart Has Eyes

Concrete Distractions

I find my imagination is either a great help or a great
hindrance to prayer or worship, depending on what I
do with it. My inner capacity to see, hear, touch, taste,
and smell are well able to receive input from the outside
material world; but even without such stimulus, my brain
does just fine at generating an entire world of experience
on its own. Often while I'm praying, my mind wanders to
the phone call I need to return, or the laundry detergent
I need to buy at the grocery store, or the conversation I'm
planning to have with a coworker the next day.

These mental wanderings are far from abstract. I can
feel the iPhone screen pressed against my cheek. I can

see and feel the color, shape, and weight of the detergent. I can smell the grocery store scents, and I can see the words *free and clear* on the label, assuring me my product is hypoallergenic. The anticipated awkwardness of tomorrow's confrontation speeds my heart rate as a surge of adrenaline washes through my body, building anxiety as I formulate my lines and rehearse responses.

I used to try and silence these distracting thoughts when trying to pray or worship, with varying degrees of failure. I felt like I needed to quiet that part of my brain constantly searching for concrete imagery so I could relate to God in mere abstractions.

"I conversed with ideas about God rather than with God Himself."

I love the way Webster defines the word abstract as *disassociated from any particular instance* and *having no pictorial representation or narrative content.*[1]

According to this definition, my life of prayer and worship used to be very abstract. I conversed with ideas *about* God rather than with God Himself, keeping my interactions with God *disassociated from any particular instance.* I was interacting with qualities associated with God rather than with the God who is Himself those qualities. I was dealing in a world of theories in a manner very much impersonal and detached, and certainly with no pictorial representation whatsoever. All of this very *abstract* interaction with God left precious little for my imagination to grip—my imagination, which was designed to latch on to the experiential, the pictorial—the concrete.[2]

Is it any wonder the thought of purchasing laundry detergent was more compelling than prayer? I was under the assumption I needed to remain imaginatively dormant in order to pray or worship. Somehow, I had come to believe proper piety demanded I bring less than my full self to God. I have since discovered this to be untrue.

> *"'Teacher, which is the great commandment in the Law?' And he said to him, 'You shall love the Lord your God with all your heart and with all your soul and with all your mind.'"* (Matthew 22:36–37)

Whatever distinctions exist between heart, soul, and mind, if I am not involving my imagination in loving God, I am loving Him with less than He deserves. What's more, there is absolutely no biblical reason not to harness the experiential capacity of my imagination in worship and prayer. In fact, there is every reason to intentionally and purposefully do just that.

The Bible is Full of Imagery
Try to read the heavenly throne room scenes in Rev-

elation 4 or Isaiah 6 and not be swept up into the sights and sounds described in such vivid detail. Old Testament battles, the Creation narrative, Nathan confronting David about Uriah and Bathsheba, Jesus touching the leper, the crucifixion and resurrection narratives, the ascension—the entire Bible is filled with an invitation to engage your inner capacity to experience biblical reality in powerful ways.

"Blessed be the God and Father of our Lord Jesus Christ, who has blessed us in Christ with every spiritual blessing in the heavenly places." (Ephesians 1:3)

When I read this verse, I no longer try to merely analyze the theological content. There's nothing wrong with theological analysis, but my imagination is sure to wander toward the exciting world of pending phone calls and grocery store trips if that's all I do. Instead, I'm learning to intentionally engage my imagination to inwardly experience what I'm reading about. What do these heavenly places look like? If I lack sufficient material for my imagination to work with, a quick perusal of Ezekiel and Revelation will solve this problem.

What would it look like for me to be surrounded by every spiritual blessing in those heavenly places? What might I see and hear? What would I sense, feel, and experience? Where am I in relation to the Father? How do

I see Him in the picture? What about Jesus? How is the Spirit at work? What is it like to receive this magnitude of blessing from my Father's hand? What does that kind of love feel like? What does His countenance right now tell me about my value and His love?

Don't make the mistake of confusing what is experienced in the imagination as being make-believe.[3] Just because my imagination is capable of envisioning fantasy doesn't mean that's all it sees. I've been to the zoo and seen, heard, and smelled real elephants. Right now, as I sit in this coffee shop and write, if I close my eyes and engage my imagination, I am able to re-experience this very real thing. I can also experience unicorns, which I've never seen and don't believe are real. My imagination can choose between fantasy and reality, and I am well able to tell the difference.

What we are talking about here is experiencing reality as defined by the Bible, which is designed to be authoritative in just this way. Scripture provides an inexhaustible array of reality for my imagination to feast upon. Even as I'm inwardly experiencing heavenly reality in Ephesians 1:4, I discover in the next chapter this isn't mere fantasy: I am, in fact, seated in this heavenly reality right now.

"But God, being rich in mercy, because of the great love with which he loved us, even when we were dead in our trespasses, made us alive together with

Christ—by grace you have been saved—and raised us up with him and seated us with him in the heavenly places in Christ Jesus." (Ephesians 2:4–6)

The Eyes of My Heart

"For this reason, because I have heard of your faith in the Lord Jesus and your love toward all the saints, I do not cease to give thanks for you, remembering you in my prayers, that the God of our Lord Jesus Christ, the Father of glory, may give you a spirit of wisdom and of revelation in the knowledge of him." (Ephesians 1:15–17)

Paul is not asking the Father to give us the Holy Spirit. Rather, he is asking God to bestow within us a new, or at least increased, capacity within our human spirit. If this prayer is answered in my life, my spirit will be characterized by both wisdom and revelation in the knowledge of Him.

These two spiritual characteristics are essential to knowing Christ. Wisdom speaks to insight and understanding; it's about principles and application. It is not exclusively abstract, but it leans more in the direction of the conceptual side of things. It is the illuminating work of the Holy Spirit that enables my spirit to perceive truth.

In addition to this, I need a spirit of revelation. The Greek word translated into the English *revelation* is *apokalupsis,* which means *unveiling.*[4] We get our word apocaplyse from it. A veil obstructs what we can see. When a veil is present, I am unable to see what is on the other side of the veil. When the veil is removed, I can now see what I could not see before; I can now experience what I could not previously access. This is not because something is there that wasn't before, but because something isn't there that was. Revelation enables me to see what was already real but unseen, because the veil has been lifted.

> *"Revelation enables me to see what was already real but unseen, because the veil has been lifted."*

The next verse begins to give us more insight into what this means:

> *"Having the eyes of your hearts enlightened ..."* (Ephesians 1:18a)

Revelation happens, not because God changes something in my eyeballs, but because He changes something in my heart. Don't think of *heart* as the muscle that pumps blood through the body. That's not how biblical writers used the term. Think of *heart* as the inner self, where the soul and spirit overlap. Paul understands that we were designed to experience some things inwardly that we are not currently experiencing in fullness, so he is praying God will change this. He is asking God to open up the eyes of our heart. The Greek word for *enlightened* is *photizo*, which means to let in light. This makes me think of a camera shutter. When you click the button, the shutter opens, letting in light and allowing an image to be seen and captured.

Revelation happens when the eyes of my heart open and the veil lifts. God's light comes in, enabling me to see and experience what I couldn't see and experience before. What does He want me to see?

"Having the eyes of your hearts enlightened, that you may know what is the hope to which he has called you, what are the riches of his glorious inheritance in the saints, and what is the immeasurable greatness of his power toward us who believe, according to the working of his great might that he worked in Christ when he raised him from the dead and seated him at his right hand in the heavenly places." (Ephesians 1:18–20)

Calling. Inheritance. Power.

This is all about identity. He wants us to have a clear inward perspective of who we are, whose we are, what our purpose is, and what heavenly resources are at our disposal. This is more than theology, though it certainly is that. This is not mere abstraction; God wants us to experientially and relationally know Him in a revelatory manner. These are things in the heavenly realm we remain oblivious to, apart from revelation. He doesn't just want us to know we are seated in heavenly places. He wants us to sit there, look around, and take in the view. He doesn't just want us to know conceptually we are surrounded by every spiritual blessing in this place; He wants us to take inventory. He wants us to live from that place.

Removing the Veil

"*Now the Lord is the Spirit, and where the Spirit of the Lord is, there is freedom. And we all, with un-veiled face, beholding the glory of the Lord, are being transformed into the same image from one degree of glory to another. For this comes from the Lord who is the Spirit.*" (2 Corinthians 3:17–18)

This may be one of the most important passages in the Bible. It doesn't just tell us we ought to be transformed into the image of Christ, it tells us how this is to happen. How are we to experience real and lasting freedom? First and foremost, this kind of change happens through connection with God's presence. "Where the Spirit of the Lord is, there is freedom."

Note that this does not say: *Where the doctrine of God's*

omnipresence is affirmed, there is freedom. God is fully present in every place. Few believers would fail to affirm this doctrine and yet freedom is not the result. But the *experience* of God's presence brings freedom to captives; that kind of transformation can occur no other way.

Previously in this chapter, Paul has been referencing a familiar story from the Old Testament. Moses went up on the mountain and met with God. As a result of this encounter, when Moses came down off the mountain, his face was shiny—so shiny they covered his face with a veil. It must have been freaking people out.

The veil served to hide the glory that came through divine encounter. On this side of the veil, God's people were unable to see the glory of God even though it was present.

Of course, the idea of a veil functioning in this way is a much broader biblical theme, reaching beyond this story and this example. Both in the Tabernacle and in the Temple there was a veil, separating God's people from experiencing the manifest presence of God within the Most Holy Place. It served as a concrete metaphor for the breech between God and Man, created when Adam and Eve were exiled from Eden.

"Not like Moses, who would put a veil over his face so that the Israelites might not gaze at the outcome of what was being brought to an end. But their minds

were hardened. For to this day, when they read the old covenant, that same veil remains unlifted, because only through Christ is it taken away. Yes, to this day whenever Moses is read a veil lies over their hearts. But when one turns to the Lord, the veil is removed." (2 Corinthians 3:13–16)

Though God's people were able to read the old covenant, they were unable to enter the Holy of Holies.

"...they couldn't see because they could not see."

Though they could read, learn, and apply the Law, they remained separated from knowing God, from seeing His glory. Their minds were hardened. This doesn't just mean stubbornness. It means they couldn't see because they *could not see.*

Christ came to solve this exact problem. Through Christ, the veil can be removed, the way can be opened. No longer are God's people limited to a life of principles and application void of His presence. The veil is lifted. All we have to do to begin entering into this experiential life in God's presence is turn to Christ. It is in daily turning to Christ that we continue to live in this way.

Let's look again at 2 Corinthians 3:18, this time in the New King James Version:

"But we all, with unveiled face, beholding as in a mirror the glory of the Lord, are being transformed into the same image from glory to glory, just as by the Spirit of the Lord." (2 Corinthians 3:18, NKJV)

All who have turned to Christ now have access to experience His presence and see His glory, for the veil has been removed. But we see His glory *as in a mirror.* What could this mean? I look in a mirror in order to see what I look like. When I see Christ's glory, it will tell me something about myself, because there is something about Jesus' identity that is the key to my own.

In the Disney film *The Lion King*, Simba gazes into the pool's reflection and sees his father's face. I believe this passage is painting a similar picture. When the veil lifts and I gaze upon the glory of Christ, I do so as though looking in a mirror. When I see what is true about Christ, I discover what is true about me.

Is Jesus God's Son? Then I am a son too. Is Jesus righteous? Then I have been made righteous in Him. Is Jesus God's heir? Then I am a co-heir. Is Jesus seated at the Father's right hand? Then I am there, in Him. These things are not simply doctrines to be read and affirmed, they are an invitation to see, an invitation to know. They are an invitation to experience. As my friend Yancy Smith says so well, they are *a menu that invites us to feast.*

What will be the result of eating this meal? We will be transformed into the image of Christ. When we experience the glory of Christ, we will discover what has been made true about our position in Christ. This revelation will transform us from the inside out so our condition begins to come into alignment with our position. As Dutch Sheets says, we *become who we are*.[2] Paul tells us they covered Moses' face in order to hide that the glory was fading away with the passage of time. When we are transformed, however, the glory of Christ in us will not fade as the glory faded from Moses' face; instead, this process ever escalates, from *glory to glory*.

Lust and fear, both fairly universal struggles, are understood within this context as simply the enemy's counterfeit. Through both lust and fear, our enemy invites us to inwardly experience tomorrow's pleasure or pain in vivid transforming power, thus bending the eyes of our heart toward things it was never intended to see and experience. What a freeing thing it is when we discover this inner cinema was designed to show another movie altogether. Freedom isn't when we merely quit thinking the things that shouldn't be thought. Freedom is when we begin to see the things we were meant to see, from God's perspective.

Beyond Just Saying My Prayers

"Let us then with confidence draw near to the throne of grace, that we may receive mercy and find grace to help in time of need." (Hebrews 4:16)

If I close my eyes and inwardly turn to Christ, I have access to a heavenly reality, glorious beyond description. I can see the veil, torn top to bottom, with a glorious light beaming through the frayed seam, beckoning me to come inside. As I step through, I am swept up in a scene that all at once both bludgeons my senses and soothes my every fear. On the throne is the King, the Ancient of Days. The elders are prostrate on their faces before the Holy One, their crowns scattered before Him, flung down from them lest any glory but His glory receives honor. The hosts of heaven worship Him. Six winged angels fly about and sing of His holiness. On the throne, I see God clothed in light. His glory fills the Temple. At once, I am undone. At once, I am at home.

With confidence, I draw near.

This, or something very much like it, is often what is occurring inside me when I attend the weekend services at my church and participate in corporate worship. By fully engaging my inward capacity to see, I am bringing my whole self—not just my religious behaviors—to God in worship. I recognize a religious life of reading, learning, and doing is thoroughly insufficient. The heavenly reality Jesus sacrificed Himself to grant me access to is now mine to see and know. Anything short of this kind of relationally experiential life with God would fail to adequately appropriate what Jesus has provided.

5

Conforming to the Age to Come

Starting Life Together

Nancy and I met and became friends during our junior year of high school. Our college choices led us our separate ways for a number of years, but just before her senior year of college our paths crossed again. This time we fell in love, and decided to get married.

Engagement is an interesting time, when two are committed to a relationship they have not yet consummated. There is a constant tension between *now* and *tomorrow*. During engagement, there is giving and receiving—but with limitation. Yet the experience of giving and receiving prior to marriage hints at the reality to come.

Then there is the planning. As our wedding approached, more and more of our present became consumed with preparation for that day. But more than this, our lives began to intertwine. Our schedules began to overlap as we found every excuse to be together. We were not married, but began to communicate before marriage in ways that anticipated the life together we were moving toward. We began to share resources and steward finances in increasing partnership. We began blending individual aspects of our lives while we were still two, because we were moving toward the moment we would become one. We experienced bits and pieces of tomorrow, today.

Becoming parents is similar. Soon after our wedding, Nancy and I decided to begin having children. This decision about tomorrow changed everything before anything really changed. Even our intimacy took on a whole new flavor as we anticipated the maybes and the what-ifs. Suddenly, we noticed every cute little baby carried by every exhausted parent in every place. A quick glance shared between us would communicate a world of reality as we dreamed of what might be for us one day.

But more changed for us than a simple eagerness for what was not yet. We began to change in the present because that future reality was becoming real to us in that season. As our thoughts and hearts began to orbit around children not yet born, they seemed to revolve around ourselves less than they had before. Old selfishness began to fade, and previously common conflicts became increasingly rare. We were different, because we had begun to live today in light of tomorrow.

Anticipation

Anticipation is a powerful thing. It is that moment when the present is shaped by what is yet to come, when our now is influenced by our tomorrow. N.T. Wright describes this as the future breaking in upon the present.[1] We experience this in all kinds of ways, big and small, positive and negative. For my children, the entire month of December is shaped by the anticipation of Christmas morning. Sometimes this anticipation helps them. Sometimes, not so much.

Boys play at being men, girls at being women. Preteen girls experiment with makeup. A young man with a clear vision of one day becoming a doctor labors to earn the grades now that will take him there then. Our consumer credit system is entirely built upon spending money now we anticipate earning later. Our consumer credit reporting system is built entirely upon the assumption that past and present performance always predicts future reality.

What we anticipate now has a significant impact not only on the present, for the things we do now in anticipation of the future actually shape our future in powerful ways. This tendency we have to live today in light of tomorrow is part of what it means to be human. It is something we must steward well, for fear or despair about tomorrow will certainly lead us astray. Faith, on the other hand, gives us a glimpse of God's vision of tomorrow enabling us to live now in light of what is not yet.

This idea is illustrated even in the biblical view of measuring days:

"God called the light Day, and the darkness he called Night. And there was evening and there was morning, the first day." (Genesis 1:5)

Don't we intuitively understand a day's beginning in terms of morning and its end as night? And yet the Bible reverses this from the very beginning. Scripture seems to get this backward. Or is something very subtle about the way God wants us to understand time hidden within the creation narrative?

God has set things up so that we begin tomorrow, today. As the sun is setting on today, we begin to experience tomorrow. Tomorrow begins at midnight, long before tomorrow ever dawns in glorious sunrise. Sabbath, the seventh day, the day of rest, begins at sundown on Friday night. On Friday God's people work all day; but Friday evening, before Saturday has arrived, Sabbath begins. We experience *now* what is *not yet*. We anticipate.

When Christ, who is Sabbath's fulfillment, returns,

everything will be set right. Everything will be made new. But before dawn breaks in upon us, even before the sun sets on our present age, we are invited in all kinds of ways to begin to experience and live from that reality now. It is still Friday, but for us, Saturday has already begun.

This anticipation is more than merely a conceptual awareness, in the present, of a future reality. We don't simply live now with an expectation that someday things will change. We anticipate the future moment, when New Creation will bring renewal to all the earth, as we experience and become conduits of New Creation now. We are in this age but we are not of this age. We do not see this age from the perspective of this age; we see this age from the perspective of the age that we now belong to—the age to come. N.T. Wright says it this way:

> ... From one point of view, the day has already dawned, while from another it's still on the way ... He is like someone taking off just as dawn is breaking and flying rapidly westward, catching up with the end of the night and arriving in the new country in time to experience dawn all over again. His body and mind know it's already daytime, while the world around him is still waiting for the dawn to break. That is the picture of the Christian, living in the new day of God's kingdom—a kingdom launched by Jesus—while the rest of the world is still turning over in bed.[2]

The question will always be raised: how much of that future reality can we expect to experience in the present?[3] Some use the *now/not yet* concept to attempt to lower our expectations. This is only possible if we use the *now/not yet* framework from the perspective of the present—here and now, we look toward the future New Creation reality and ask how much we should expect to experience now. Then we take inventory of our experience (or lack thereof) in the present age and determine we must not be able to experience much New Creation now.

This line of thinking misses the point entirely. The *now/net yet* framework is not designed to think of *then* from the perspective of *now*. Rather, we are to think of *now* from the perspective of *then*. When I truly begin to see myself as part of that future reality instead of the present one, I ask a different kind of question. How much of this future reality that I am now fully connected to, can I release into this present evil age? I'm not living now, hoping to make it to then. I'm living then already—in the now.

The only limiting factor is the level of my connection with that future reality. The only limit is the limitation of my sight. As far as my eyes can see, God will give.

The boundaries of Abraham's future inheritance were limited only by his capacity to see.

"*For all the land that you see I will give to you and to*

your offspring forever." (Genesis 13:15)

Be Transformed

"I appeal to you therefore, brothers, by the mercies of God, to present your bodies as a living sacrifice, holy and acceptable to God, which is your spiritual worship. Do not be conformed to this world, but be transformed by the renewal of your mind, that by testing you may discern what is the will of God, what is good and acceptable and perfect." (Romans 12:1–2)

In the last chapter, we explored Paul's understanding of spiritual transformation from 2 Corinthians 3:17-18. Transformation results from an unveiling, a revelation; revelation produces change. Paul gives us a glimpse into what God reveals that produces change in us. God reveals the glory of Christ, and in so doing shapes our identity. I am transformed into the image of Christ when the Holy Spirit enables me to see and understand with the eyes of my heart what I could not see before.

Transformed is a key word in 2 Corinthians 3:18, and here in Romans 12:2. The Greek word *metamorphoo* is a combination of two distinct words or ideas. The first, *meta*, refers to a change of condition or location. The second, *morphoo*, means to shape or to form something.[4] These two words together present us with a very strong image of being shaped or formed in a manner that changes my condition, my location, or both.

How am I to be transformed in this way? I experience transformation through the renewal of my mind. This renewal is not a reset; it is not another version of the same mind. This is a qualitative renewal—a new sort of thing, rather than a new version of the same sort of thing. I will be shaped and formed in a manner that changes my condition and/or my location when my mind is changed into an altogether different sort of mind. This refers to an entirely new perspective: a new way of perceiving and a new way of processing what is perceived, with entirely new categories of both thought and conclusion. To borrow Bob Hamp's excellent and precise way of articulating this truth, we are to *think differently,* not just *think different.*[5]

And how am I to experience this inward transformation, this renewal of the mind? Paul answers us by telling us what it doesn't mean.

"*Do not be conformed to this world.*" (Romans 12:2a)

"Our mind is renewed as it becomes conformed to the age to come."

The Greek word behind the English *world, aion,* is better translated as *age* instead of *world.*[6] There's a perfectly good Greek word for *world, kosmos,* and Paul didn't elect to use it. Why translators sometimes insist on *world* over *age* is explained when we understand what is meant by each word in this case.

World, in Paul's sense here, doesn't mean *planet.* What the translators mean by *world* is the present state of affairs on our planet, the current system under which our planet operates. We see translators using the same word *world* for the Greek *aion* again in this passage:

> *"In their case the god of this **world** has blinded the minds of the unbelievers, to keep them from seeing the light of the gospel of the glory of Christ, who is the image of God."* (2 Corinthians 4:4, emphasis added)

Paul is referring to Satan himself, calling him the *god of this world.* The Greek word is *aion.* It refers to one period of time, distinct from other periods of time. But this is also how the translators are using the English *world.* Satan is the *god of this world* and he has influence and power over the present state of affairs. Implied strongly in this kind of language, whether we use *age* or *world,* is the certain hope that this state of affairs will not be allowed to stand indefinitely. Satan may be the god of this age within our world, but one day the eternal God will come and set things right.

Going back to Romans 12:2, we see Paul is giving us

a significant clue regarding the renewal of our minds. Remember—we experience transformation when our mind is qualitatively renewed. Paul tells us how this does NOT happen: it doesn't happen when our minds are conformed to the present age, the present state of affairs on our planet, the current system dominated by darkness. If our mind is not to be conformed to the present age, what is the other available option? The age to come. Our mind is renewed as it becomes conformed to the age to come. We are transformed, made qualitatively new, as we begin to perceive and experience life from the perspective of the age to come.

The Kingdom of God

The Jewish people during the time of Christ lived with an acute and pervasive sense of the distinction between the present age and the age to come. N.T. Wright makes this distinction clear:

> "The present age was a time when the creator god seemed to be hiding his face; the age to come would see the renewal of the created world. The present age was the time of Israel's misery; in the age to come she would be restored. In the present age wicked men seemed to be flourishing; in the age to come they would receive their just reward. In the present age even Israel was not really keeping Torah perfectly, was

*not really being YHWH's true humanity; in the age
to come all Israel would keep Torah from the heart.[7]*

The people of Israel were longing for the age to come,
for the time when God would set everything right. This
hope was expressed through a variety of words and ideas
like *the day of the Lord, the resurrection of the dead, the
coming of the Son of Man,* and *the Kingdom of God.* Things
were presently a big mess, but they were longing for the
day when the Kingdom of God would be established.

When Paul challenges us to not be conformed to the
present evil age, but instead be made qualitatively new
by the renewing of our mind, he is actually challenging
us to anticipate New Creation, to begin tomorrow today,
to allow our minds to be conformed in the present to the
age to come. We can see this *age to come* vision expressed
in John's vivid description of the new heavens and earth:

*"Then I saw a new heaven and a new earth, for the
first heaven and the first earth had passed away, and
the sea was no more. And I saw the holy city, new
Jerusalem, coming down out of heaven from God,
prepared as a bride adorned for her husband. And
I heard a loud voice from the throne saying, 'Behold,
the dwelling place of God is with man. He will dwell
with them, and they will be his people, and God
himself will be with them as their God. He will wipe*

away every tear from their eyes, and death shall be no more, neither shall there be mourning, nor crying, nor pain anymore, for the former things have passed away.' And he who was seated on the throne said, 'Behold, I am making all things new.' Also he said, 'Write this down, for these words are trustworthy and true.'" (Revelation 21:1-5)

In this passage, we find a New Testament expression of this same Jewish longing for the age to come; for the time when present suffering will end because God, by His very presence with His people, will make all things new. This is New Creation imagery and language at its very best, and it is important for us to catch the defining characteristics of how New Creation will happen in the age to come.

In verse four, John writes *the former things have passed away.* Then in verse five, he records God's declaration *I am making all things new.* How does New Creation happen? God causes old things to pass away and He makes all things new. New Creation is the essential characteristic of the age to come.

This understanding has significant bearing upon how we understand Paul's challenge to *be transformed through the renewal of our minds* in Romans 12. What might it mean for us in the present moment to begin to have our mind shaped by a reality in which old things are gone and everything is made new? What might it be like for us to begin to live today in anticipation of that future reality? If that *not yet* time is truly when God's Kingdom will be established, what would it look like for us to live in the present as citizens and ambassadors of that Kingdom? What if an age where there are no tears, death, mourning, crying or pain was to begin, through us, to invade the present evil age where there is little else?

Jesus taught us to pray, "*Your kingdom come, your will be done, on earth as it is in heaven.*" (Matthew 6:10)

God has called us to live exactly this way, as citizens of the age to come.[8] We are ambassadors of New Creation, conduits of the Kingdom of God through whom God's restoration can flow. Anticipating what is not yet, we release New Creation within the present as we live now from the perspective of then. This way of understanding who we are in Christ is not some obscure biblical theme; rather, it's the very heart of what the gospel does.

> "*Therefore, if anyone is in Christ, he is a new creation. The old has passed away; behold, the new has come.*" (2 Corinthians 5:17)

What God will one day do in all the world (see Revelation 21:4-5), He is doing now in and through us in anticipation of that future day (see 2 Corinthians 5:17).

A Down Payment

I recently purchased a car from my step-dad. He needed to sell and I needed to buy, so it was a good opportunity for both of us. We agreed on a price and a plan for me to make an initial down payment, take possession of the vehicle, and then spread the rest of the payments across the following four months.

This sort of financial scenario is familiar to all of us. We certainly understand credit in our culture! The function of a down payment is also well known to us: a down payment is something provided in the present, serving to guarantee future payments.

Can you imagine if I had shown up to make the original down payment and handed him money from one of the board games in our game closet? I can promise you I wouldn't have driven away in the car. Why? Because the clear expectation for the down payment was real money he can spend now, even while the money serves to guarantee future payments. Take a look at how Paul uses the word *guarantee* in this verse:

> *"In him you also, when you heard the word of truth, the gospel of your salvation, and believed in him, were sealed with the promised Holy Spirit, who is the guarantee of our inheritance until we acquire possession*

of it, to the praise of his glory." (Ephesians 1:13–14)

Here we see a terrific example of the dynamic tension between the present age and the age to come, between the now and the not yet. We have heard the gospel. We've believed. We've been sealed. This is all part of our present experience. But an inheritance remains. There remains an *until we acquire possession* ahead of us in the future. But we are not left to wait for this promised inheritance with empty hands and hearts. He has given us a down payment. The word translated into the English word *guarantee* is actually a Hebrew word, *arabon*, transliter-

"The Kingdom will come; and yet the Kingdom is presently among us, within us, by the Spirit."

ated into the Greek. It means *down payment*.

In the following two passages you can see this same idea expressed:

"And it is God who establishes us with you in Christ, and has anointed us, and who has also put his seal on us and given us his Spirit in our hearts as a guarantee." (2 Corinthians 1:21–22)

"For while we are still in this tent, we groan, being burdened—not that we would be unclothed, but that we would be further clothed, so that what is mortal may be swallowed up by life. He who has prepared us for this very thing is God, who has given us the Spirit as a guarantee." (2 Corinthians 5:4–5)

What has God given us as a down payment? He has given us Himself: the Spirit is our guarantee in the present of our inheritance in the future. And by the Spirit we, in the present, are empowered to live today in anticipation of what is to come. On that day, when God's new city descends, Creation will be made new, all the old things will be removed: Heaven and Earth will occupy the same space, overlapping and interlocking in ways unimaginable to us now, and God will live among His people.

But God does not require us to hope for that great day while living disconnected from it. By the Spirit, He dwells with us now. As the Spirit fills and empowers us, that future reality becomes a present experience. There is a wedding day still to come, and the ring He has given is precious indeed.

The Kingdom will come; and yet the Kingdom is presently among us, within us, by the Spirit.

"For the kingdom of God is not a matter of eating and drinking but of righteousness and peace and joy in the Holy Spirit." (Romans 14:17)

"Nor will they say, 'Look, here it is!' or 'There!' for behold, the kingdom of God is in the midst of you." (Luke 17:21)

So, we hope.

We long.

We wait eagerly for that which is not yet.

And yet, that future reality is already present within us. We pray. We serve. We love. We see old things passing away, and we experience the renewing work of New Creation in the present by the Spirit. We begin tomorrow, today.

"Your kingdom come, your will be done, on earth as it is in heaven." (Matthew 6:10)

6

New Lenses

A New Perspective

On our way to church, our family typically drives by a beautiful piece of land owned by Ross Perot. It's really a spectacular place, with lush green pastures spreading out over rolling hills upwards toward the horizon. The Circle T Ranch comprises thousands of acres. It's not unusual to see a camel, or even a few bison. Most often, though, you can see hundreds of Angus beef cows grazing. They are beautiful, black, and seemingly unaware of their fate. One day as we were driving by, Teddy, my eight-year-old son, commented from the back of the car.

"Wow, look at all those bulls."

"Those are cows, Teddy, not bulls. They are girl cows,

not boy cows," Mom replied. "They keep the boy cows, the bulls, in a different pasture."

There was a quiet pause. We could almost hear the gears in Teddy's head grind as he processed this information. He has noticed the calves peppered throughout the pasture, next to, as he now understood, their mothers.

"If they keep the bulls somewhere else, how do they have baby cows?"

Awkward pause.

"That's a very good question, Teddy. Dad, would you care to answer?"

I was still reeling from the implications of Teddy's question. He clearly knows more about the birds and bees, or, as in the present case, the bulls and cows, than I realized. I'm quite certain he doesn't really understand the mechanics of it all; but clearly, he knows you have to have a mommy and a daddy to produce the obvious result. I needed a real, albeit incomplete, answer, and I needed it quick.

"Well, you see son, they do, sometimes, let the bulls in to where the cows are, but only for a little while. The boy cows tend to annoy the girl cows."

His sisters, both teenagers, attempted to suppress their laughter.

Teddy glanced to his right, then his left, at his sisters on either side. He then nodded, in complete understanding.

Teddy is still at the age where boys and girls are annoyed by each other. He has some female friends, but his tolerance for them (and theirs for him) is fairly short-fused. Girls are still a mystery to him; not the kind of mystery that evokes exploration, just the kind that elicits bewilderment and avoidance. There are times when he seems genuinely disgusted by the fairer sex. This seems fairly reciprocal.

But there will come a day when all this will change. There will be a girl. He will suddenly see the female half of our species from a totally new perspective. Likely, she will have been there all along, just without his notice. Then, an epiphany: he will see her as never before, and he will never be able to see her in the same way again. This change—and this is the point—won't be because she is different today than yesterday. She hasn't changed that fast! The change will be within Teddy; he will see her differently than he has before. He will see her from a new perspective. (I'm hoping this doesn't happen for a while.)

Transfiguration

"And after six days Jesus took with him Peter and James and John, and led them up a high mountain by themselves. And he was transfigured before them, and his clothes became radiant, intensely white, as no one on earth could bleach them. And there appeared to them Elijah with Moses, and they were talking with Jesus."

(Mark 9:2–4)

This wonderful story from the gospels is shocking on so many levels. Talking to the dead was generally discouraged for Jews, so likely unexpected for Jesus' three friends. Talking to the dead is generally thought impossible in post-enlightenment western culture, so likely inexplicable for your average contemporary reader. I haven't heard many sermons from this passage.

But as I've come across this account (which also appears in Matthew and Luke), I've mostly been struck by the change in Jesus' appearance. Suddenly, Peter, James, and John saw Jesus as they had never seen Him before. (It's no wonder John recognized Him so many years later on the isle of Patmos; see Revelation 1:12-17.)

"The veil lifted, and they were enabled to see Jesus from a heavenly perspective."

Something changed, but what? They saw Jesus differently, but did Jesus change, or did their way of seeing Jesus change? I guess I've always assumed the former. But in examining the passage, I am increasingly convinced of the latter. They saw Elijah and Moses—this implies the disciples were enabled to see into the spiritual realm. From the text, we can infer a shift in the disciples' capacity to perceive, from the natural into the supernatural, from the earthly to the heavenly. At the same time, they saw Jesus differently, strongly indicating not a change in Jesus Himself, but rather a change in how they saw Jesus.

From an earthly perspective, I'm sure they were quite accustomed to seeing Jesus as a typical Jewish man in his early thirties: hands calloused from years of manual labor, face weathered from the sun, clothes, feet, and sandals grey from the dust of the Galilee. That's how they had always seen Him. But on this day, they saw Him differently; seeing earth from the vantage point of heaven will do that. For a brief moment they saw Jesus now from the perspective of then, here from the perspective of there.

The Greek word translated *transfigured* in Mark 9:2 is *metamorphoo*. Outside of the three gospel accounts of Jesus' transfiguration, it only appears twice in the New Testament. One of these instances we examined in Chapter 4, another we looked at in Chapter 5.

"But we all, with unveiled face, beholding as in a mirror the glory of the Lord, are being transformed into the same image from glory to glory, just as by the Spirit of the Lord." (2 Corinthians 3:18, NKJV)

"Do not be conformed to this world, but be transformed by the renewal of your mind, that by testing you may discern what is the will of God, what is good and acceptable

and perfect." (Romans 12:2)

The Greek word *metamorphoo* is where we get the English word *metamorphosis*; you probably remember it from biology class. It is used to describe the transformation a caterpillar goes through in becoming a butterfly. It's a very specific kind of change that goes way beyond mere modification. A butterfly is a completely different sort of thing than a caterpillar. I find it intriguing this is the same word used in these three passages in different and yet related ways.

In 2 Corinthians 3:18 *metamorphoo* is translated *transformed* and refers to the change we experience when the veil lifts (revelation) and we are enabled to see what we couldn't see previously. This is essentially what happened to the disciples in Mark 9:2. The veil lifted, and they were enabled to see Jesus from a heavenly perspective. In Romans 12:2, *metamorphoo* is also translated *transformed*, and refers to the change we experience when our mind (our total way of thinking) is renewed as it becomes conformed to the age to come.

We can also see this aspect of *metamorphoo* in Mark 9. When the veil lifted and Jesus' three closest friends were enabled to see Jesus as never before, they saw Him from the perspective of the age to come. They saw Him then as John would later see Him on Patmos, as all of us will see Him on that Day.

In the last chapter, we talked about the importance of seeing now from the perspective of then. In this chapter, I want to discuss the significance of seeing here (earth) from the perspective of there (heaven). Both of these ideas are packed into the concept of New Testament transformation.

The Intersection of Heaven and Earth

"In the beginning, God created the heavens and the earth." (Genesis 1:1)

From the very beginning, we see the reality God has created comprised of both earth and heaven. Biblically, the idea of heaven includes not just the sky and universe, but also the heavenly (non-material) realm. There is a duality within created reality that includes both. How we think about heaven and earth can make a big difference in how we think about everything. Let's take a look at two common misconceptions.

- **Materialism**

Materialism is the view of earth that denies heaven. This can be philosophical, when one supposes matter (and energy, a form of matter) is all that exists. Or it can be pragmatic, when one lives as if matter is all that matters, so to speak, perhaps even while affirming the existence of more. One view denies there is anything other than matter; the other denies significance to anything beyond the material world. We live within a very materialistic culture, and by this I mean both definitions.

Materialism, as a philosophy, denies God, the supernatural, miracles, and anything outside of natural cause and effect. This view of reality, beginning with philosophy, has trickled down from academia into pop culture via art, science, and even theology. Most people from the West, like myself, have a very deeply ingrained assumption that *there must be a natural explanation* in reaction to even the appearance of the supernatural.

Materialism, as a functional way of living, may conceptually affirm that God (or god, gods, or some kind of spiritual reality) exists, while living as if He doesn't. Heavenly reality is acknowledged when pressed, but life is lived as if Earth exists alone. Indeed, men may even attend church or participate in some kind of religious activity, but this routine is relegated to a separate and independent category that encroaches very little, if at all, on the rest of life.

Sadly, as it often does, theology has adapted to our materialistic culture. As discussed above, *deism* affirms a transcendent God (other than us, over us) who is distant and uninvolved in the natural world. There is no supernatural.

Cessationism is the somewhat popular view that the power gifts of the Holy Spirit (healing, miracles, tongues, prophecy, etc.) passed away with the conclusion of the apostolic age and the closing of the scriptural canon. This view affirms both God's transcendence (other than us, over us) and His immanence (near to us, involved with us) while reducing our expectation of experiencing God's immanence by relegating the vast majority of God's supernatural activity to biblical times. God doesn't do such things any more. They are unpopular these days, after all.

- **Natural/Supernatural Dualism**

  The natural/supernatural view, though still misleading, is vastly superior to materialism. This view firmly holds to both God's transcendence and immanence. Earth is real, but heaven is a real place too. Though the natural world still almost always operates by natural cause and effect, God occasionally intervenes in supernatural ways when it suits His purpose. With a more extreme version of this set of lenses, one might even look for, and acknowledge, a great amount of supernatural intervention within the natural world. But the natural and supernatural remain two independent categories of reality; they certainly do not share the same space. Miracles happen, but they happen within a reality that is normally not miraculous. The supernatural is real, but it happens within a world not fundamentally supernatural in its nature.

  In Christianity, this view of things produces an understanding of the gospel more likely to emphasize going to heaven when you die rather than experiencing heavenly reality in the here and now. The spiritual is reserved for then; the material is our present reality. Jesus' provision will be understood merely as God's method of getting us to heaven rather than as God's provision to restore heaven upon earth. We are most likely to read the New Testament and assume we will leave earth and spend eternity in heaven

> *"A miracle is God's activity within creation to restore broken creation to His original design."*

rather than noticing that ultimately, heaven comes to earth and they both wind up being the same place (see Revelation 21).[1] I am convinced that this way of seeing things is largely influenced in Western culture by philosophers like Plato, and later by the *gnostics*, who maintained a similar dualistic view of heaven and earth, with the spiritual seen as *good* and the natural seen as *bad*.

When this kind of dualism forms the lenses through which we see reality, we can't help but relegate the supernatural to 1) the future, when we all die and go to heaven, or 2) an independent reality to which we have limited, if any, access. God occasionally reaches across the void, but we have no expectation of co-laboring with God in such matters. Through this lens, we will definitely not see the separation of heaven and earth as a bad thing, the very problem Jesus came to solve, the very heart of the good news of His proclamation that the Kingdom of Heaven is here.

An Integrated View

"In the beginning, God created the heavens and the earth. The earth was without form and void, and darkness was over the face of the deep. And the Spirit of God was hovering over the face of the waters. And God said, 'Let there be light,' and there was light." *(Genesis 1:1–3)*

And God said ...

Creation *ex nihilo* (Latin: from nothing) is an important tenet of orthodox Christianity. The material world, with its origin in nothing save the mind of God, is deeply imbedded in scripture from the very beginning.

When John began his account of New Creation in Christ, he begins in similar fashion.

"In the beginning was the Word, and the Word was with God, and the Word was God. He was in the beginning with God. All things were made through him, and without him was not any thing made that was made." (John 1:1–3)

While a good deist (believing in God as sort of a cosmic watch maker who is no longer involved in the operation of the watch) might affirm all of the above, they could never affirm what John says just a few verses later.

"And the Word became flesh and dwelt among us, and we have seen his glory, glory as of the only Son from the Father, full of grace and truth." (John 1:14)

And certainly not this:

*"Long ago, at many times and in many ways, God spoke to our fathers by the prophets, but in these last days he has spoken to us by his Son, whom he appointed the heir of all things, **through whom also he created the world.** He is the radiance of the glory of God and the exact imprint of his nature, **and he upholds the universe by the word of his power.** After making purification for sins, he sat down at the right hand of the Majesty on high."* (Hebrews 1:1–3, emphasis added)

A fully biblical view of reality will not only affirm the existence of both heaven and earth (seeing heaven as spiritual and the earth as merely natural), it will see the earth as fundamentally spiritual, not just in its origin, but also in its current state. The natural has its origin in, and is currently sustained by, the Word of God. Everything is essentially spiritual, both the material and the non-material. The natural is supernatural. This makes the *super* superfluous. Everything material is spiritual, though what is spiritual is not always material.

At this point we risk so deconstructing the miraculous that it vanishes as a concept. If everything is a miracle, then nothing is. We must be careful to redefine what we mean by a miracle. In the previous view of things, a miracle is God's intervention, from the supernatural realm into the natural realm. If everything in its origin and existence is something spiritual, then a miracle is no longer simply supernatural. The supernatural goes away as a category, but miracles remain. Within this new context, what is a miracle?

Let me define it this way: a miracle is God's activity within creation to restore broken creation to His original design.

Healing is a miracle. Expelling demons is a miracle. Forgiving a sinner is a miracle. Bringing the dead (whether physically or spiritually) to life again is a miracle. Calming a storm is a miracle. Man exercising dominion over earth is a miracle (turning water to wine, walking on water, etc.) because, from the beginning, that was God's design for creation.

The importance of this shift cannot be overstated. When we define the miraculous according to the dualistic view described above, we cannot help but see the miraculous as something outside the norm, something we do not expect to happen. On the other hand, when we define the miraculous from within the integrated approach, we see the miraculous as completely normal and normative, the thing God is always doing in sustaining and restoring Creation.

In the Garden of Eden

Once you begin to see reality through these lenses, you will begin to notice all kinds of things in scripture your previous set of lenses filtered out.

"And out of the ground the Lord God made to spring up every tree that is pleasant to the sight and good for food. The tree of life was in the midst of the garden, and the tree of the knowledge of good and evil." (Genesis 2:9)

I know what trees look like. I know what fruit trees produce. I spent a year in Honduras as a child, and have very fond memories of mangos. About three miles from home, just as the river snaked around in a giant U shape, right in the middle of the U, there was a grove of enormous mango trees. The branches halfway up the tree were thick enough to lie down and take a nap on without fear of falling. I spent some amazing afternoons in that tree with a knife and saltshaker. Green mangos with salt are amazing.

I've eaten fruit from trees. I've climbed trees. I've planted trees. I've even cut down trees. In all my experience with trees, I've never seen a single tree that produced knowledge as a fruit; or life either, for that matter. Genesis 1-3 describes a reality for us that seems very foreign: what kind of place is it where you can see knowledge and taste life? Where demons take on physical form? Where angels guard the path home?

From the very beginning, it appears that heavenly and earthly realities, though distinct in some ways, overlap one another in ways that defy comprehension for us. It appears that the ability to see the overlap between heaven and earth, to interact naturally in both realms, is, at least partly, what was lost when Adam and Eve sinned.

The Gateway to Heaven

"Jacob left Beersheba and went toward Haran. And he came to a certain place and stayed there that night, because the sun had set. Taking one of the stones of the place, he put it under his head and lay down in that place to sleep. And he dreamed, and behold, there was a ladder set up on the earth, and the top of it reached to heaven. And behold, the angels of God were ascending and descending on it! And behold, the Lord stood above it and said, 'I am the Lord, the God

of Abraham your father and the God of Isaac. The land on which you lie I will give to you and to your offspring.'" (Genesis 28:10–13)

"And he was afraid and said, 'How awesome is this place! This is none other than the house of God, and this is the gate of heaven.'" (Genesis 28:17)

A pivotal moment in Jacob's life involved a brief glimpse into unseen reality through a dream. And what does he see? Heaven and Earth, connected, intersecting, and overlapping, with angelic beings moving in and out of both realms. This is a key moment theologically in the development of Jewish thought, for *the house of God* is now equated with a revelation of this intersection of heaven and earth.

Your Kingdom Come

"Your kingdom come, your will be done, on earth as it is in heaven." (Matthew 6:10)

The Fall of Man due to sin includes not only Man's disconnection with God spiritually (spiritual death) but also a limitation in his capacity to see and interact with the heavenly realm. At the heart of God's plan to act within Creation to restore His world to His design is a desire to restore the influence of heaven upon the earth. This is reflected in the heart of the prayer Jesus taught us to pray. We see this same idea elsewhere in scripture.

During His famous nighttime conversation with Nicodemus in John 3, Jesus says the following:

> *"Jesus answered him, 'Truly, truly, I say to you, unless one is born again he cannot see the kingdom of God.'"* (John 3:3)

Similarly, in verse five He uses the phrase *enter* the Kingdom of God to describe the outcome of being born again. If we view these verses through the old lenses, we can easily assume Jesus is simply talking about going to heaven when we die. But that's not actually what He says. He says as a result of being born again, a person will be able to see and enter the Kingdom of God (Matthew calls it the Kingdom of Heaven). Jesus' entire preaching ministry is summed up in the declaration that because of Jesus, this realm, the Kingdom of God, is now among us.

What got broken at the Fall? Among other things, our capacity to see and interact with heavenly reality. What did Jesus promise would result from being born again, from above? This capacity will be restored.

New Heaven and New Earth

This idea is powerfully communicated in a passage we

have previously examined.

> *"Then I saw a new heaven and a new earth, for the first heaven and the first earth had passed away, and the sea was no more. And I saw the holy city, new Jerusalem, coming down out of heaven from God, prepared as a bride adorned for her husband. And I heard a loud voice from the throne saying, 'Behold, the dwelling place of God is with man. He will dwell with them, and they will be his people, and God himself will be with them as their God. He will wipe away every tear from their eyes, and death shall be no more, neither shall there be mourning, nor crying, nor pain anymore, for the former things have passed away.' And he who was seated on the throne said, 'Behold, I am making all things new.' Also he said, 'Write this down, for these words are trustworthy and true.'"* (Revelation 21:1–5)

In Revelation 21, we find in the end, the prayer Jesus taught us to pray is answered—big time. Heaven comes to earth, resulting in God's will being done upon the earth, displacing all that is not His will. Old things pass away. Everything is made new.

New Creation.

God powerfully works to restore Creation to His design; every miracle up to this point was simply pointing us constantly forward to this, the ultimate miracle. That design, and by extension God's redemptive goal, is to once again merge heavenly and earthly reality. Heaven comes to earth. God dwells among His people. Heaven and earth are the same place.

The right set of lenses changes how we see everything.

7

Seated in Heavenly Places

The Tabernacle and Temple

Think back to Genesis 28—the story of Jacob we discussed earlier. In the dream he was given a revelation of heaven and earth, connected by a ladder upon which angels moved in and out of both heavenly and earthly realities. He woke from this dream and declared that place to be the *house of God*. This concept is extremely important in the Jewish mind. What is the *house of God*? It is the place where God's presence is experienced.

It is the place where heaven and earth intersect and interact.

In his book *The New Testament and the People of God*, N.T. Wright makes this statement: *In the mainline Jewish worldview ... the heavenly and the earthly realms are distinct but closely intertwined.*[1]

He gives further clarification in his later work *Jesus and the Victory of God*:

The symbolism of the Temple was designed to express the belief that it formed the centre not only of the physical world but also of the entire cosmos, so that, in being YHWH's dwelling-place, it was the spot where heaven and earth met.[2]

These ideas are firmly imbedded in the biblical accounts of both Tabernacle and Temple.

> *"And you shall put the mercy seat on the top of the ark, and in the ark you shall put the testimony that I shall give you. There I will meet with you, and from above the mercy seat, from between the two cherubim that are on the ark of the testimony, I will speak with you about all that I will give you in commandment for the people of Israel."* (Exodus 25:21–22)

> *"Then the cloud covered the tent of meeting, and the glory of the Lord filled the tabernacle. And Moses was not able to enter the tent of meeting because the cloud settled on it, and the glory of the Lord filled the tabernacle. Throughout all their journeys, whenever the cloud was taken up from over the tabernacle, the people of Israel would set out. But if the cloud was*

not taken up, then they did not set out till the day that it was taken up. For the cloud of the Lord was on the tabernacle by day, and fire was in it by night, in the sight of all the house of Israel throughout all their journeys." (Exodus 40:34–38)

"As soon as Solomon finished his prayer, fire came down from heaven and consumed the burnt offering and the sacrifices, and the glory of the Lord filled the temple. And the priests could not enter the house of the Lord, because the glory of the Lord filled the Lord's house. When all the people of Israel saw the fire come down and the glory of the Lord on the temple, they bowed down with their faces to the ground on the pavement and worshiped and gave thanks to the Lord, saying, 'For he is good, for his steadfast love endures forever.'" (2 Chronicles 7:1–3)

More than a mere structure built for worship and religious activity, the Jewish Temple was the house of God. It was the place where God, a spiritual being who lives in the heavenly realm, dwelt among His people in manifest glory. It was the place where heaven and earth intersected; it was the place where heaven and earth were one.

In Genesis 1-3, we see a world where heaven and earth intermingle and intertwine in mysterious and powerful ways. We see a place where trees produce knowledge and life and where God walks in the cool of the day. Due to sin, Man is exiled from this reality, and an angel guards the way back. In Revelation 21 we see the fulfillment of God's redemptive plan, when heaven and earth are joined once more. In between, before God has fully unfolded His plan of redemption, the place where heaven and earth continue to intersect is the Temple.

Prior to Jesus' death and resurrection, the house of God was a man-made structure. It was a portable Tabernacle made of animal hides until Solomon constructed a magnificent structure, eventually destroyed at the time of the Babylonian conquest.

In the New Covenant, the Temple is still considered the place where God dwells with His people in manifest presence, the place where heaven and earth intersect, the place where heaven and earth are the same place. But now, the Temple is not a man-made structure.

"Do you not know that you are God's temple and that God's Spirit dwells in you?" (1 Corinthians 3:16)

"Or do you not know that your body is a temple of the Holy Spirit within you, whom you have from God? You are not your own." (1 Corinthians 6:19)

"What agreement has the temple of God with idols?

For we are the temple of the living God; as God said, 'I will make my dwelling among them and walk among them, and I will be their God, and they shall be my people.'" (2 Corinthians 6:16)

"So then you are no longer strangers and aliens, but you are fellow citizens with the saints and members of the household of God, built on the foundation of the apostles and prophets, Christ Jesus himself being the cornerstone, in whom the whole structure, being joined together, grows into a holy temple in the Lord. In him you also are being built together into a dwelling place for God by the Spirit." (Ephesians 2:19–22)

"As you come to him, a living stone rejected by men but in the sight of God chosen and precious, you yourselves like living stones are being built up as a spiritual house, to be a holy priesthood, to offer spiritual sacrifices acceptable to God through Jesus Christ." (1 Peter 2:4–5)

Don't miss the significance of this: as a believer, you are now the *house of God*. You are the place where God, who lives in heaven, dwells upon earth. You are the place where heaven and earth are the same place. That was always God's design. When all He has provided in Jesus' victory is fulfilled, it will be so. This is the prophetic longing of scripture.

> "*They shall not hurt or destroy in all my holy mountain; for the earth shall be full of the knowledge of the Lord as the waters cover the sea.*" (Isaiah 11:9)

> "*For the earth will be filled with the knowledge of the glory of the Lord as the waters cover the sea.*" (Habakkuk 2:14)

Revelation 21 describes the day when the New Jerusalem descends to earth and the earth is reborn as *old things passing away and everything being made new.* This is the essence of New Creation. When Creation happened, heaven and earth overlapped and God dwelt among His people. When New Creation happens, this reality is restored.

What about you? Right now?

> "*Therefore, if anyone is in Christ, he is a new creation. The old has passed away; behold, the new has come.*" (2 Corinthians 5:17)

What God intended from the beginning, what He will one day do in all the earth, He is doing in and through you now. You are His Temple, His Tabernacle, the place where His glory dwells, the place where heaven and earth intersect; the conduit through which heaven can invade earth and accomplish His purposes in the here and now, in advance of Jesus' return.

In the Tabernacle, God's presence was manifest as a pillar of fire and cloud. Look at the events of Acts 2 through that lens for a moment.

> "*When the day of Pentecost arrived, they were all together in one place. And suddenly there came from heaven a sound like a mighty rushing wind, and it filled the entire house where they were sitting. **And divided tongues as of fire appeared to them and rested on each one of them**. And they were all filled with the Holy Spirit and began to speak in other tongues as the Spirit gave them utterance.*" (Acts 2:1–4 emphasis added)

You were never designed to follow religious rules or to learn biblical principles and try hard to obey them. You were designed to live as the intersection of heaven and earth, and to carry the presence of God wherever you go. You are called to New Creation. This is how heaven sees you. Heaven sees you here, from the perspective of there. Heaven sees you now, from the perspective of then.

Peter, James, and John got a glimpse of Christ from this perspective. What if you were to get a heavenly glimpse of who you really are? It would change everything for you. The old things would pass away. Everything would be new.

Seated in Heavenly Places

This is the very perspective Paul invites you to share.

"*But God, being rich in mercy, because of the great love with which he loved us, even when we were dead in our trespasses, made us alive together with Christ—by grace you have been saved—and raised us up with him and seated us with him in the heavenly places in Christ Jesus, so that in the coming ages he might show the immeasurable riches of his grace in kindness toward us in Christ Jesus.*" (Ephesians 2:4–7)

What is the nature of this wonderful salvation God has provided for us in Christ? He has *made us alive together with Christ.* We were dead. He has made us alive again. This is what it means that we *have been saved.* That would be enough, but it's not all: He has also given us a share in the exaltation of Christ, in that He has *raised us up with Him and seated us with Him in the heavenly places in Christ Jesus.*

We may think of this in one of two ways. One possibility is this: since I am currently on earth, and this passage tells me I am also seated in the heavenly places in Christ Jesus, I am currently occupying two different places at the same time. I am on earth in a material sense, but also located in heaven spiritually. But how might I understand this verse through the lens of the Jewish heaven and earth worldview, embodied in the Temple? From this perspective, I understand this passage to be saying not that I am now located in two distinct places—but rather that those two places are now the same place within me.

Understanding this perspective on heaven and earth makes a huge difference in how you see yourself. Heaven isn't some far away place you will cross over to once your heart stops beating. Heaven, the non-material realm of God's reign, intersects with the material realm within you. You are the point of intersection, the place of overlap. In Christ, you are positioned as the conduit through which heaven can invade earth and the realm of God's reign can extend into the earthly sphere.

This is the shape of the prayer Jesus taught us to pray.

> *"Do not be like them, for your Father knows what you need before you ask him. Pray then like this: 'Our Father in heaven, hallowed be your name. Your kingdom come, your will be done, on earth as it is in heaven. Give us this day our daily bread, and forgive us our debts, as we also have forgiven our debtors. And lead us not into temptation, but deliver us from evil.'"* (Matthew 6:8–13)

Our Father in heaven

We begin with a revelation of who God is and where God is (the heavenly realm).

Hallowed be your name

We continue by acknowledging God's plan is not about us; it's about Him and His glory.

Your kingdom come

Then we command the kingdom to come. The grammar of this verb is very specific. This is a command not a request. We are to pray like this: *Kingdom of God, come!* We command it to move from where it is to where it is not. What else could *come* possibly indicate?

Your will be done, on earth as it is in heaven

This statement (also a command) further unpacks the previous. We declare that the will of God, currently done in heaven, be done on earth where it is currently not being done.

The rest of the prayer simply lists for us the various ways we will see the answer to this prayer expressed: provision, forgiveness and healed relationships, holiness, freedom, and the defeat of evil.

We can see God's design for earth and heaven to overlap, and understand how this design has been distorted due to sin. Once we see that God's plan of redemption is aimed at restoring His design, we see the gospel in a new light. We see ourselves as never before. This presents us with a significant challenge: seeing ourselves differently is not always an easy shift to make.

The Obstacle of Unworthiness

It may be no problem to recognize *we were dead in our trespasses,* but it may prove quite a stretch to see ourselves seated on the throne of heaven in Christ at the right hand of the Father. On one hand, this simply brings us back to a much earlier point—our need for and complete dependence upon revelation. The scriptural information (we are seated in heavenly places) does not itself give us this new perspective. We need the Holy Spirit to open the eyes of our heart, to enable us to see what we couldn't see before. His illuminating work alone can produce this result.

On the other hand, there may actually be a barrier to our capacity to receive this revelation. A revelation of God's holiness is often accompanied by a keen awareness of our lack of it.

> "*In the year that King Uzziah died I saw the Lord sitting upon a throne, high and lifted up; and the train of his robe filled the temple. Above him stood the seraphim. Each had six wings: with two he covered his face, and with two he covered his feet, and with two he flew. And one called to another and said: 'Holy, holy, holy is the Lord of hosts; the whole earth is full of his glory!' And the foundations of the thresholds*

shook at the voice of him who called, and the house was filled with smoke. And I said: 'Woe is me! For I am lost; for I am a man of unclean lips, and I dwell in the midst of a people of unclean lips; for my eyes have seen the King, the Lord of hosts!'" (Isaiah 6:1–5)

"Then one of the seraphim flew to me, having in his hand a burning coal that he had taken with tongs from the altar. And he touched my mouth and said: 'Behold, this has touched your lips; your guilt is taken away, and your sin atoned for.'" (Isaiah 6:6–7)

Though Isaiah was initially very aware of his unworthiness, he was also willing to immediately receive God's cleansing touch, symbolized by the coal from the altar.

But this is often the step we don't take. When faced with divine encounter, we become aware of our unworthiness. God's desire is to bring us into a place where we are confident in His cleansing; instead, we maintain our distance even as we maintain our position of unworthiness.

A debilitating sense of unworthiness is a clear and common obstacle to truly seeing and embracing our heavenly position in Christ. When I examine my own worth, I will always judge myself unworthy. When I examine my own righteousness, I will always find poverty and lack in this area, for I have no righteousness of my own. But this is the very good news of the gospel, isn't it? Though I have no righteousness of my own, God provides a righteousness that is not my own.

"And be found in him, not having a righteousness of my own that comes from the law, but that which comes through faith in Christ, the righteousness from God that depends on faith." (Philippians 3:9)

The most anti-gospel thing we can do is to attempt to establish our own righteousness.

"For, being ignorant of the righteousness of God, and seeking to establish their own, they did not submit to God's righteousness." (Romans 10:3)

Seeking to establish our own righteousness fails to recognize the wondrous exchange we receive by faith through which Jesus' own righteousness is imputed to us.

"For our sake he made him to be sin who knew no sin, so that in him we might become the righteousness of God." (2 Corinthians 5:21)

If I discover an inward hesitancy to fully embrace my position in heavenly places in Christ, and in examining this I find a sense of unworthiness at its root, then what

I have uncovered is a deeper problem. My problem isn't simply that I struggle to embrace my position in Christ; my problem is that I am still basing my standing with God on my own righteousness.

How do I know this is the case? Because it is my own righteousness I am evaluating. How else would I come to the conclusion that I am unworthy? It is apparent if I were evaluating not my own, but Christ's righteousness, I would come to a different conclusion altogether: righteous, holy, worthy.

If this resonates with you, if you find you hesitate to boldly and confidently embrace your position in Christ at the right hand of the Father in heaven due to a sense of your own unworthiness; if this very fact points you to the reality that it is your own performance, your own righteousness you must be evaluating in order to come to this conclusion, then your struggle is deeper than you can possibly imagine. For what gospel have you believed if it is based on seeking to evaluate and establish your own righteousness?

If this is the case, you stand in need of revelation. You need the Holy Spirit to open your eyes to see a reality that already exists, but to which you are, and have been, blind. First, you need a revelation of Jesus' finished work on the cross. He has already made complete provision for your sin. Secondly, you need a revelation of Jesus' righteousness imputed to you on the basis of faith alone. When the

Spirit opens the eyes of your heart to this reality, you will see with great clarity that God is no longer evaluating your performance at all: He is evaluating Jesus' performance, and His alone. It is Jesus' righteousness being examined, not yours. Jesus' righteousness has been imputed to you. Your standing with God, your position in Christ, rests solely upon that basis.

If you have had any other basis than this, today is a day to ask for revelation. Ask for the gift of repentance, the grace to see differently than you have before and to align with what God has declared to be true in His gospel.

When I refuse to see myself seated with Christ in heavenly places and judge myself unworthy, I have judged Jesus' blood to be insufficient and God's word to be untrue. This is not humility. It is arrogance of the highest order to judge as inadequate what God has judged to be of ultimate sufficiency.

Christ in Me

Following from the revelation that I am in Christ and my position before God has been secured based on the merit of Christ alone, is the truth that any hope I have of walking in alignment with that reality day by day is dependent upon Christ being in me. That I am in Christ is a change of position. That Christ is in me transforms my condition.

What is the mystery of the gospel that God has now

revealed? *Christ in you, the hope of glory.*

> *"To them God chose to make known how great among the Gentiles are the riches of the glory of this mystery, which is Christ in you, the hope of glory."* (Colossians 1:27)

I first heard the gospel when I was five years old. My mom, recently born again herself, shared with me the story of Jesus' death and resurrection. Even at an early age, by God's grace, I had an awareness of my need for forgiveness. When she shared with me that Jesus wanted to come live inside my heart, I just knew I wanted Him to do that. I received His free gift and invited Him to come live inside my heart. He did.

I am in Christ. Seated at the right hand of the Father—in Christ. This positional change took place immediately when I first believed. At that same moment, Jesus came and took up residence within my heart. Christ is in me. My only hope of experiencing on earth who I already am in heaven depends completely on Jesus living in me and through me.

> *"I have been crucified with Christ. It is no longer I who live, but Christ who lives in me. And the life I now live in the flesh I live by faith in the Son of God, who loved me and gave himself for me."* (Galatians

2:20)

My only hope that my condition could grow to match my position is that I would share in His nature. This transformation of my condition is not instantaneous. Though Jesus' indwelling presence by His Spirit is immediate, the inward transformation by which I become conformed to His image takes place over time. But the power that transforms is not my effort to change, but rather His nature expressed within me.

> "*By which he has granted to us his precious and very great promises, so that through them you may become partakers of the divine nature, having escaped from the corruption that is in the world because of sinful desire.*" (2 Peter 1:4)

My position before God changes the moment I respond to the gospel with faith, the moment where I fully rely upon Christ alone and receive the full provision of His finished work. In that same moment, I am born again and I am privileged to share in God's nature. I experience transformation from the inside out as I learn to fully yield to His inward presence day by day.

How Do I See Others?
Seeing things from Heaven's vantage point gives me

a new perspective on both God and myself, but it also changes how I see others.

> *"From now on, therefore, we regard no one according to the flesh. Even though we once regarded Christ according to the flesh, we regard him thus no longer." (2 Corinthians 5:16)*

When Paul prays in Ephesians 1 that God would open the eyes of our heart, one of the things he wants us to see is Christ's inheritance in the saints.

> *"Having the eyes of your hearts enlightened, that you may know what is the hope to which he has called you, what are the riches of his glorious inheritance in the saints."* (Ephesians 1:18)

When I look at my brothers and sisters in Christ, do I see them according to the flesh? When I see others according to the flesh, I see physical appearance, natural abilities, social standing, family status, limitations, weaknesses; I see them from an earthly perspective.

But how does heaven see them? They are God's Temple, the place where God dwells, the place where heaven and earth are the same place, the place where God's glory rests. In the day, a pillar of cloud rests upon them; at night, a pillar of fire.

After an amazing time of teaching and ministry, Jesus visited His hometown, Nazareth. He taught the people, and did mighty works there. At first they were amazed, recognizing the hand of God that was upon Him. They were recognizing the heavenly reality Jesus carried, the presence of the Spirit of God upon Him. But then their focus shifted.

> *"'Is not this the carpenter's son? Is not his mother called Mary? And are not his brothers James and Joseph and Simon and Judas? And are not all his sisters with us? Where then did this man get all these things?' And they took offense at him. But Jesus said to them, 'A prophet is not without honor except in his hometown and in his own household.' And he did not do many mighty works there, because of their unbelief."* (Matthew 13:55–58)

The perspective from which we see others, to some degree, determines what we are able to receive from them. When I choose to see others as heaven sees them, to honor what God has deposited in them and to recognize His presence in and upon them, I can more fully receive from God through them.[3] On the other hand, when I see them merely as so-and-so's son, a plumber, an attorney, or *that's just my pastor,* then by my choice of perspective, I shut myself off from what they might impart into my life. Familiarity can breed more than just contempt.

The importance of perspective is staggering. That Jesus has made a way for us to see and enter the Kingdom is of utmost importance. It is more than a theological concept that we have been raised up with Christ and seated with Him in heavenly places. Heaven is the place from which we are to live experientially: this is where the blessings are.

"Blessed be the God and Father of our Lord Jesus Christ, who has blessed us in Christ with every spiritual blessing in the heavenly places." (Ephesians 1:3)

8

Owners and Stewards

No Bad Hips in Heaven

The class was wrapping up.

For the past hour and some change, I had shared about Jesus' declaration that the Kingdom of God is present with us; God is present among us to work powerfully according to His purposes.

This class usually unleashes like a fire hydrant; more is said than can be absorbed. Some try to take notes, but this quickly becomes futile. I especially love that moment when a participant tosses his pen and note paper aside in exasperation. You can't learn your way into the Kingdom anyway, so I'm ok with that.

I taught about the Kingdom of God that night, but I

did more than talk. I invited Jesus to demonstrate His Kingdom. As I concluded my final thoughts, my heart was already turning toward what God might want to do among us.

I explained to the class of about 200 what we were about to do, and then prayed.

"Jesus, You're the King. You are our King. We don't want to just talk about Your presence and power. We welcome You here to be and do for us whatever You want to be and do."

I waited quietly.

I waited a bit more.

I felt a little twinge in my left hip. As far as Words of Knowledge go, it wasn't a ton to go on. It was a very small twinge.

I waited a bit more.

Nothing.

Nothing.

Was that God? What if it wasn't? I don't want to just manufacture something on my own. I don't want to fail. I don't want to look like a fool.

I have these internal conversations all the time.

I stepped out.

"I feel like God wants to heal someone's left hip. If that's you, if you have a left hip problem, raise your hand."

Just to my right, on the front row, a middle-aged woman nervously raised her hand. Her husband, seated next to her, looked surprised, anxious, and a bit excited all at once. I asked them both to stand.

"I'm going to pray for your hip and then I'm going to ask you to check it out. I will ask you to move it; do what you couldn't do before, ok? And then let me know what you notice." I asked her husband to place his hand on her hip.

"Hip, I command you to be healed in Jesus' name. Full range of motion be restored. I command pain to go right now, in Jesus' name."

It wasn't a long prayer.

She began to move her hip, twisting her leg, lifting her knee up towards her shoulders, back and forth. She began to smile. Her husband began to smile too.

"How's the pain now?"

"Completely gone."

"Range of motion?"

"Back to normal."

"Totally?"

"Totally."

To my left, one section over and three rows back, a man sat with his hand excitedly in the air. He also had a hip issue, but he hadn't raised his hand. He wasn't sure why. As the woman had shared about her healing, he suddenly felt something shifting in his own hip at the same time, a bit of heat and something moving around.

I asked him to stand and check things out. He was

completely healed too!

"Anyone else here tonight with a hip issue?"

Seven more people stood. I polled them: four left hips, two right hips, and a lower back problem.

I don't remember saying anything about right hips or backs, but ok. I asked them to stand and gave similar instructions about checking out pain and range of motion after I prayed. I coached them to place their attention and affection on Jesus, and His presence among us.

I invited everyone in the class to stretch out their hands toward one of these seven and pray out loud with me. I led them a bit on the kinds of things to pray:

"Speak to the issue. Command healing. Command the pain to go. Declare God's Kingdom, His presence, power, and authority in your body. Rebuke infirmity."

I prayed a short prayer, asked those standing to move around, and then polled them again.

Six were completely healed, somewhat to my surprise.

One didn't experience any improvement at all, a big guy with a left hip injury. Inwardly, I had an impression: *It's a soul issue.* Spend some time with him. I asked him to stick around after class. He just needed to forgive his dad and receive some healing in that area.

His hip was completely healed, too.

The first lady and her husband approached me at church about six weeks later to report she had just run a 5k race with no hip issues whatsoever. God is good.

There are no bad hips in heaven. Earth just became a bit more like that.

"Your kingdom come, your will be done, on earth as it is in heaven." (Matthew 6:10)

God's Plan

God owns the earth. His plan from the beginning has been for Man to steward the earth as God's representative.

An owner is the person who has possession and authority over property. To the owner belongs ultimate responsibility and accountability. A steward is not an owner. An owner delegates his authority to the steward, and the steward is accountable to the owner. He must represent the vision and heart of the owner in caring for the assigned property. The owner might limit his direct activity within the property, for he has delegated stewardship to another. He acts in and upon the property through the one tasked to represent him.

Sometimes the owner gives specific directions to the steward. Other times the steward, connected as he is to the owner's vision and heart, recognizes what needs to be done and makes decisions, not out of obedience, but out of responsibility. He has been delegated authority that he might manage the affairs of the owner in just this manner. A steward who waits passively for instructions is not a good steward. A good steward will take initiative to make sure he, as a manager, knows the owner's heart and vision, and then he moves the owner's agenda forward.

The owner's heart and vision are expressed through the activity of the steward as he exercises the authority delegated to him.

A professional baseball team works in just this manner. Nolan Ryan currently owns my local team, the Texas Rangers. John Daniels is the General Manager. There are times when John Daniels, the steward, is tasked with implementing a decision Nolan Ryan, the owner, has made unilaterally. In this scenario, the steward's task is obedience. There are other times when John Daniels himself acts unilaterally to make decisions within the scope of delegated authority he has been given. If the steward were to sit idly at his desk waiting for the owner to make all the decisions and give all the directives, he would be fired. His job is to manage. Sometimes this involves direct obedience. Often it involves initiative, leadership, and decision-making not directly defined by the owner, but as a reflection of the owner's overall vision and agenda. At other times, decisions are made collaboratively, as the owner approaches the steward with a concept, or the steward approaches the owner with a new idea. In these situations, there is discussion, sometimes pushback, and ultimately a decision. The final authority, of course, rests with the owner, but the owner is influenced by the steward and often yields to his ideas in specific matters, having confidence the steward is deeply connected to his own heart.

I believe this model is in many ways a reflection of the way God desires to relate to man.

The earth belongs to the Lord.

> "*The earth is the Lord's and the fullness thereof, the world and those who dwell therein.*" (Psalm 24:1; see also Psalm 50:12, Exodus 9:29, Deuteronomy 10:14, 1 Chronicles 29:11, Job 41:11, 1Corinthians 10:26, Psalm 89:11)

God has delegated authority in the earth to Man as a steward.

> "*The heavens are the Lord's heavens, but the earth he has given to the children of man.*" (Psalm 115:16)

> "*Then God said, 'Let us make man in our image, after our likeness. And let them have dominion over the fish of the sea and over the birds of the heavens and over the livestock and over all the earth and over every creeping thing that creeps on the earth.'*" (Genesis 1:26)

Jesus' Parables

This owner/steward model is one of the major themes of Jesus' teaching in parables.

- **The Parable of the Talents**

(Matthew 25:14-30; Luke 19:12-27)

In this well-known story, the owner gave various sums of money to three stewards with the expectation that they would do business with these resources and return a profit to the owner. Two of the servants faithfully executed their delegated responsibility and were rewarded as good stewards with increase. One servant was not faithful in his assignment, and even what he had was taken away and given to another.

- **The Parable of the Tenants**

(Matthew 21:33-41; Mark 12:1-9; Luke 20:9-16)

In this parable, the owner has planted a vineyard and leased it to tenants, who are accountable to the owner for their care of the vineyard. He sends servants to check on things and they mistreat the servants. The owner then sends his son, and the tenants kill the son. In this example of the owner/steward imagery, the owner has assigned care of property to a steward who is to be held account-able for that care. In this case, the steward is wicked, and punished as a result.

- **The Parable of the Wedding Feast**

(Matthew 22:1-14)

This parable presents us with a king who has planned a wedding feast for his son. His servants are tasked with inviting guests to the celebration. Those invited refuse to come, and then proceed to mistreat the servants. The king then reassigns the servants to bring others who had not originally been invited.

This parable is aimed at the chief priests and Pharisees, who are represented in the story as guests invited to the wedding feast but refuse to come, and then mistreat the servants sent by the king (the prophets and ultimately Jesus Himself). The imagery in the story clearly illustrates the owner/steward model represented by the king and the servants who invite the guests. Beyond this, the sharp point of this story is the chief priests and Pharisees, those given authority and influence over Judah and God's people, have not been faithful in their delegated assignment.

- **The Parable of the Prepared and the Unprepared Servants**

(Matthew 24:45-51; Luke 12:35-48)

Here, the master has put a servant in charge of his household with the responsibility of feeding his family while the master is away. His hope is that upon returning, he will be able to promote his servant to an even greater level of responsibility as a reward for his faithfulness. But if the steward is not faithful, he will be held accountable.

Each of these parables uses the owner/steward relationship as a picture to describe the relationship between God and His people. In each story, God is the owner who has delegated responsibility and authority to a steward or group of stewards. In most cases, the owner goes away but *"New Creation is the aim of God's redemptive plan."* will return at some point, at which time the stewards will give an account of their activities while the owner was gone. I don't believe this implies God is absent; rather, the steward is expected to function responsibly within the scope of his designated assignment as the owner's representative. When it is time to give an account, those who have been faithful will be rewarded with increase, those who have not will be punished and their assignment given to another.

These owner/steward parables are most directly understood as stories about the religious leaders of Israel. They had been given a stewardship from God with the expectation of fruitfulness, faithfulness, increase, etc. God had sent prophets—and ultimately His own Son—as messengers and they mistreated those messengers. They will ultimately be held accountable for this.

But these stories also point us toward a bigger picture beyond the issue of the Pharisees and chief priests of Israel. God gave stewardship of the earth to mankind, with the expectation that man would remain connected to God's heart and agenda. He expected man to represent God within the earth in a manner that moved God's agenda forward, extending His dominion in all the earth. In Genesis 3, man disconnected from God, rejected Him, and has filled the earth with something else entirely.

Many of Jesus' other parables are about God seeking and finding what was lost. Taken together, the two themes give us a clear picture of a big part of Jesus' message: man is lost, and God's plan for extending His reign in the earth through the stewardship of man has been derailed. God, in Christ, has come back to rescue man; to reconnect to him, save him and ultimately, to restore the earth to its proper place under the stewardship of man who is rightly connected to God.

God became a man to do it.

Creation and New Creation

In the Icon Productions movie *The Passion of the Christ*, there is a poignant moment where Jesus, stumbling under the weight of the cross, looks up at Mary, his mother, and says *See, I am making all things new.*

New Creation is the aim of God's redemptive plan. The Bible begins with Creation. In Genesis 3, we come to understand why God's good Creation is now less than it should be. The rest of the Bible is the story of the unfolding of God's redemptive plan, culminating ultimately in Jesus, and to be fulfilled completely when Jesus returns, heaven comes to earth, and the earth is reborn.

The earth is longing for redemption.

> *"For the creation was subjected to futility, not willingly, but because of him who subjected it, in hope that the creation itself will be set free from its bondage to corruption and obtain the freedom of the glory of the children of God."* (Romans 8:20–21)

Creation is longing for New Creation. The work of New Creation has already been done through Jesus and His finished work; the reality of New Creation will come to complete fulfillment when Christ returns. In between, New Creation is already bursting upon the scene in and through those who are in Christ.

> *"Therefore, if anyone is in Christ, he is a new creation. The old has passed away; behold, the new has come."* (2 Corinthians 5:17)

What God will one day do in all the earth, He is doing now, in and through you and me. The two are linked together: New Creation in me, New Creation in the earth. The earth is longing to be free from futility and corruption, and to obtain *the freedom of the glory of the children of God.*

"For the creation waits with eager longing for the revealing of the sons of God." (Romans 8:19)

God's desire to restore the earth under the stewardship of man serving as His representative is linked to God restoring man who has been lost. Before man can govern the earth rightly as God's steward, man must be brought back into right relationship with God.

God's solution is elegant and mysterious and wonderful and beautiful.

He became a man.

Christ died that mankind might be reconciled to God. In doing this, Christ became the last Adam. Authority over both heaven and earth has been delegated to Him. Those who believe are now *in Christ,* and Christ is in them. He is the head and they, His body. He is currently working in them to bring New Creation, causing the old to pass away and the new to come. He is currently working through them to bring New Creation into their sphere of influence, thus restoring them to their rightful place as God's stewards in the earth. One day Christ will return, and this plan of redemption will be brought to complete fulfillment in Christ.

Christ Is All, and Is In All

On earth as it is in heaven.

This phrase, the heart of the prayer Jesus taught us to pray, packs up all of the ideas we've been examining. God desires that heaven and earth be rejoined. He is restoring man as the steward through whom He governs the earth. He is reconciling man to God, reconnecting man with His own heart and life, and through man, extending His reign within Creation. He is doing all of this in and through Christ, God who became man, God who is man. He is doing all of this through you and me, who carry the presence of Christ, and are in Christ.

Everything is summed up in Christ.

"That he worked in Christ when he raised him from the dead and seated him at his right hand in the heavenly places, far above all rule and authority and power and dominion, and above every name that is named, not only in this age but also in the one to come. And he put all things under his feet and gave him as head over all things to the church, which is his body, the fullness of him who fills all in all." (Ephesians 1:20–23)

"He is the image of the invisible God, the firstborn of all creation. For by him all things were created, in heaven and on earth, visible and invisible, whether

thrones or dominions or rulers or authorities—all things were created through him and for him. And he is before all things, and in him all things hold together. And he is the head of the body, the church. He is the beginning, the firstborn from the dead, that in everything he might be preeminent. For in him all the fullness of God was pleased to dwell, and through him to reconcile to himself all things, whether on earth or in heaven, making peace by the blood of his cross." (Colossians 1:15–20)

"As a plan for the fullness of time, to unite all things in him, things in heaven and things on earth." (Ephesians 1:10)

"Here there is not Greek and Jew, circumcised and uncircumcised, barbarian, Scythian, slave, free; but Christ is all, and in all." (Colossians 3:11)

Stepping Into God's Plan

I began this chapter with a fun story about healing. If it is true God wants to do in and through me right now what He will ultimately do in all the earth (cause the old to pass away and make all things new); if it is true this expresses God's restoration of the owner/steward model of governing creation; and if it is true God's way of doing this is to put me in Christ and to place Christ in me, then, in stepping out that day to pray for some injured hips, I was stepping into the plan of God. Anytime I, as a steward, recognize and step into God's activity, I become a co-laborer—a conduit through which heaven can invade earth to restore it to His original design, and I am stepping into the very thing I was created for.

You were made for the same thing. It's not just about healing hips. It's about all the great variety of ways God makes things new.

> "*And he came to Nazareth, where he had been brought up. And as was his custom, he went to the synagogue on the Sabbath day, and he stood up to read. And the scroll of the prophet Isaiah was given to him. He unrolled the scroll and found the place where it was written, 'The Spirit of the Lord is upon me, because he has anointed me to proclaim good news to the poor. He has sent me to proclaim liberty to the captives and recovering of sight to the blind, to set at liberty those who are oppressed, to proclaim the year of the Lord's favor.' And he rolled up the scroll and gave it back to the attendant and sat down. And the eyes of all in the synagogue were fixed on him. And he began to say to them, 'Today this Scripture has been fulfilled in your hearing.'*" (Luke 4:16–21)

How does God make things new? He does it in and

through Christ. He anoints with His Spirit. He gives good news to those who desperately need it. He sets captives free. He opens blind eyes, whether physical or spiritual. He removes heavy burdens from the oppressed, and tells people all about the arrival of God's goodness and grace in restoring all things. As we see in the passage, this was fulfilled that day in Christ; and in Christ, it can find expression and manifestation through my life and through yours.

How Much Can We Experience Now?

In Chapter 5, we talked about the present age and the age to come, about God's desire for me to see *now* from the perspective of *then*. In Chapters 6 and 7, we talked about heaven and earth, about God's desire for me to see *here* from the perspective of *there*. In this chapter, we have discussed the owner/steward model for expressing God's reign upon the earth, and the plan of redemption to restore fallen man to this stewardship in and through Christ, God who became man.

None of these things will be fully realized until Christ returns. But God's expectation and desire is that we would begin to live in the here and now from the perspective of these realities. As we begin to live this way, the age to come begins to invade the present evil age, heaven begins to reshape earth, old things pass away and new things come as new creation happens in and through our lives.

The obvious question is: how much of *then* should we expect to experience *now*? How much of *there* should we expect to experience *here*? Exactly how much should we, as stewards, expect to see God's new creation agenda move forward in and through our lives prior to Christ's return?

One extreme would be to relegate the coming of God's kingdom entirely to the time following Christ's return. The other extreme would be to expect every single old thing to pass away and every single thing to be made new prior to Christ's return. The former locks us in passivity and escapism, and the latter sets us up for disappointment and minimizes the significance of Christ's return.

The reality is we simply don't know how much of *then* is possible *now*.[1] As stated in Chapter 5, our current level of revelation regarding the age to come may be our only limit. The owner has given us a sum, and He expects us to do business and produce increase as His stewards. The sower has sown the seed of His word, and expects 30-fold, 60-fold, and 100-fold increase. How much is possible? I'm not quite sure, but I expect a lot more fruitfulness is possible than we are currently seeing. What will determine the limit? From both the owner/steward parables and the soil/crop parables, it would seem the limiting factors are faith and obedience.

Ultimately, we must begin to step out of passivity, comfort, and unbelief into a place of faith and obedience where we are contending for all Jesus has provided. What we have not experienced before is irrelevant; that's the problem, not an excuse for not embracing the solution. It is also a non-issue that we don't know the limit of what is possible prior to Christ's return. We will be held accountable for what

"We will be held accountable for what we've done with what we've been given."

we've done with what we've been given, for our faithfulness with it.

Outcomes and results are still dependent upon God, for the authority is simply delegated from Him to us. The power is His, not ours. He is the owner and we are His servants.

Conclusion

With the eyes of our heart we've begun to see the present age from the perspective of the age to come, earth from the perspective of heaven, and ourselves as stewards in relationship with the Owner. We no longer define miracles as the invasion of the supernatural within a non-supernatural world. Instead, we are beginning to see all Creation as supernatural, and the miraculous as God's activity within broken Creation to bring about New Creation.

To live this kind of life will require God's presence and power.

9

Indwelt and Empowered

Didn't See that Coming

It took me completely off guard.

I was thirteen years old, attending a James Robison conference in Bedford, Texas with my mom and some of her friends. It was the first of that sort of thing I'd ever been to. I remember very few details about the conference itself, but I remember the atmosphere: it was electric with excitement. There was a palpable hunger for God in the air, and it was contagious.

I don't really remember what the message was about. But I do remember God's presence in that place. It felt thick, weighty, warm, happy, and inviting all at the same time. As we worshipped and listened to someone teach the Bible, I remember sensing His presence more and more throughout the evening.

After the message, I made my way down to the front, feeling I needed to respond somehow. The sanctuary of the host church had a darkly stained wooden kneeling rail that wrapped around the curved platform, the kind where there's room on the other side for the minister to pray for you or serve the communion elements or something like that. The lights were dimmed, and the pianist was playing something soft and reflective, worshipful.

I knelt.

At that moment, kneeling at the altar, I wasn't really sure why I had gone forward. I didn't know exactly what I hoped to receive. But it felt like God wanted to do something. I wanted that, whatever it might be.

There were a few moments of silence. Is there a certain way I'm supposed to kneel? I stole a quick glance to my right and left, noticing there were others kneeling too. They clearly knew what they were doing. They all had their eyes closed, looking slightly upward, with an especially holy look on their face. They all had their elbows resting on the rail, with their hands crossed in front of them, palms upward. I quickly attempted to mimic their posture.

She came up behind me suddenly, laid her hands on my shoulder and began to pray out loud with great intensity—in tongues.

I didn't know it was tongues. At that time, I didn't know there was such a thing as tongues, and I certainly had never heard anyone speak in tongues before. I thought I might have recognized her voice, so I peeked over my shoulder. Sure enough, it was my mom's friend Jeanne. She had also led some of the singing that day.

"It felt like heat. It felt like electricity."

I resumed my posture.

She kept praying. I wondered: *What is she saying? I don't recognize the language. I didn't know she spoke another language. I didn't ...*

All of a sudden, somebody dumped a big bucket of warm oil on my head. I felt it pouring through my hair, down my face, and over my shoulders. I couldn't help opening my eyes and wiping my hands over my face to scrape some of the oil away.

There was no oil.

At least there wasn't any I could see with my eyes or touch with my hands. But I could feel it all the same. It felt good, like tangible love. If healing is a tangible thing, that's what it feels like.

Before long, remaining upright required more and more concentration. It's not as if the room was spinning or anything like that. It's hard to describe. I was just struggling to stay up on my knees.

So I didn't.

I remember falling over, landing on my side. It was a softer landing than I anticipated. I don't know if Ms. Jeanne or someone else caught me or not. I lay there quietly for a few moments, and then it happened. From deep within I began to feel this thing inside, from my belly, rising up toward my head. It felt like heat. It felt like electricity. It felt like power. I had no idea what was about to happen. It seems like I could have stopped it if I wanted to, but I didn't want to.

By the time it rose to my mouth, it felt like joy, so I let it out. It was laughter. I began to giggle. It was this deep, raucous, uncontrolled belly laugh. It was God, but it wasn't all God. It was God's joy expressed in laughter. It was also me getting tickled at myself for behaving this way in church. Those two dynamics seemed to perpetuate one another in a dance, with God taking the lead and my self-awareness just following right along.

It was glorious.

It was healing at a level I didn't even know I needed.

I didn't speak in tongues; that came a year later at youth camp. But I got filled up with God that day. The biblical term for my experience is *The Baptism in the Holy Spirit.*

That Sunday, I walked into my seventh grade Sunday School class with a story to tell, but our church was part of a denomination that really wasn't into that sort of story. I was unaware of this dynamic, and just dove in and told the whole thing. My teacher's eyes got bigger and bigger the more I told. I interpreted this as excitement, so I just raised the intensity even higher. I talked about the lady praying in another language. I talked about the bucket of oil you could feel but not touch or see. I talked about falling down. I talked about the forty-five minute belly laugh. I told the whole thing.

The next week our family went looking for a new church. We had been asked to find a new place to worship.

I noticed a couple of immediate results from my encounter with God that day. Mainly, I felt an overall sense of peace and abiding joy I hadn't ever known before. Secondly, I began to notice a desire and ability to explain the Bible to others. As I began to do this more and more, I noticed it really seemed to help people experience God for themselves.

The Indwelling Spirit

"Jesus answered, 'Truly, truly, I say to you, unless one is born of water and the Spirit, he cannot enter the kingdom of God. That which is born of the flesh is flesh, and that which is born of the Spirit is spirit. Do not marvel that I said to you, "You must be born

again." The wind blows where it wishes, and you hear its sound, but you do not know where it comes from or where it goes. So it is with everyone who is born of the Spirit." (John 3:5–8)

The theological term is *regeneration*, which means *new birth*. In this passage, the English phrase would be *born again*. The Greek word *anothen,* translated *again,* can be taken either of two different ways, and I believe both are part of Jesus' meaning here. *Anothen* can either refer to place or time. If referring to time, this adverb can mean either *from the first* or *again.* Translators have elected to go with this meaning, probably seeking to match the context, where Jesus will, in a moment, compare this experience of spiritual birth with natural birth. Thinking chronologically, *again* is a good translation, because this spiritual birth happens after natural birth.

But this adverb can also be used in reference to place, not just time. When *anothen* refers to place, it means *from above.* This is the most direct meaning of the word, and also works very well contextually. In this same passage, Jesus contrasts Nicodemus' limited and natural earthly perspective with Jesus' heavenly perspective, pointing out Nicodemus is unable to understand Jesus because he doesn't share Jesus' heavenly point of view.

"Truly, truly, I say to you, we speak of what we know,

and bear witness to what we have seen, but you do not receive our testimony. If I have told you earthly things and you do not believe, how can you believe if I tell you heavenly things? No one has ascended into heaven except he who descended from heaven, the Son of Man." (John 3:11–13)

When speaking of the new birth, I believe Jesus has both of these meanings firmly in mind. Our first birth is insufficient; we must be born again. Being born of the earth is also insufficient; we must be born from above. Whether speaking of time or place, *again* or *from above,* Jesus uses *born of the Spirit* to describe this experience

This second birth (referring to time), where we are born from above (referring to place), results from the activity of the Spirit in our lives.

Life as a result of God's Spirit indwelling man is a powerful biblical theme. As we look at the following verses, it will be helpful to note in both Hebrew (*ruach*) and Greek (*pneuma*), the words for *wind, breath,* and *spirit* are the same.

"Then the Lord God formed the man of dust from the ground and breathed into his nostrils the breath of life, and the man became a living creature." (Genesis 2:7)

"The Spirit of God has made me, and the breath of the Almighty gives me life." (Job 33:4)

"Then he said to me, 'Prophesy to the breath; prophesy, son of man, and say to the breath, Thus says the Lord God: Come from the four winds, O breath, and breathe on these slain, that they may live.'" (Ezekiel 37:9)

"It is the Spirit who gives life; the flesh is no help at all. The words that I have spoken to you are spirit and life." (John 6:63)

"For the law of the Spirit of life has set you free in Christ Jesus from the law of sin and death." (Romans 8:2)

"But if Christ is in you, although the body is dead because of sin, the Spirit is life because of righteousness." (Romans 8:10)

"Thus it is written, 'The first man Adam became a living being'; the last Adam became a life-giving spirit." (1 Corinthians 15:45)

"Who has made us competent to be ministers of a new covenant, not of the letter but of the Spirit. For *the letter kills, but the Spirit gives life."* (2 Corinthians 3:6)

"And when he had said this, he breathed on them and said to them, 'Receive the Holy Spirit.'" (John 20:22)

When someone hears the gospel and responds with faith, they are born again, born from above. They receive eternal life. Both of these words are important. *Eternal* refers to perpetual time, but not just perpetual; this word also refers to future time. It refers to the age to come. Remember how God wants us to live *now* from the perspective of *then*? How do we do this? When we believe, God gives us life that is eternal. It is from that age, according to the age to come. It is important we understand the life we receive is life according to the age to come.

"To live without this kind of life is to not be truly alive at all."

There are a few Greek words that can be translated *life*.[1] *Bios* refers to earthly life, in the sense of the duration of our life and the earthly matters that concern it. Words like *biology* and *biography* are derived from this Greek word.

Psuche refers to the life of the soul, in the sense of the self, the person, and the inward life of feelings, thoughts, and desires that often drive us. *Psuche* is often translated *soul,* when not translated *life.* Words like *psyche* and *psychology* are derived from this word.

Neither of these words are the kind of eternal life we receive when we are born again from above. This kind of life is *zoe*—God's kind of life.[2] This is the kind of life that makes us truly alive. To live without this kind of life is to not be truly alive at all. It is not a life that is simply a span of time within which we physically function upon the earth–*bios.* It is not the kind of life rooted solely in self and driven by what I think, feel, and want—*psuche.* *Zoe* is the kind of life that only comes when we are deeply connected to God as our source. This is the kind of life God gave Adam in Genesis 2:7; Adam became not just a soul, but a living soul.

> "*Then the Lord God formed the man of dust from the ground and breathed into his nostrils the breath of life, and the man became a living creature.*" (Genesis 2:7)

God warned Adam and Eve that if they ate from the Tree of the Knowledge of Good and Evil, they would die. Death is the absence of life. What kind of life did Adam and Eve lose that day? They didn't lose their earthly life—not that day; though decay entered the world and the duration of *bios* life became limited. They didn't lose their soul life that day; their *psuche* life took over. Man became driven by what he thinks, feels, and wants, with self as his ultimate source.[3] What Man lost that day was his deep connection to God as his source—his *zoe* life.

This life-giving connection with God by His indwelling Spirit is what was lost in Eden when Man sinned, and it is this kind of life Jesus came to restore to us. Jesus came to give us eternal life—life according to the age to come, life that results from a deep connection to God through His indwelling Spirit.

> "*The thief comes only to steal and kill and destroy. I came that they may have life and have it abundantly.*" (John 10:10)

> "*For the gate is narrow and the way is hard that leads to life, and those who find it are few.*" (Matthew 7:14) "*For the bread of God is he who comes down from heaven and gives life to the world.*" (John 6:33)

> "*But whoever drinks of the water that I will give him will never be thirsty again. The water that I will give him will become in him a spring of water welling up to eternal life.*" (John 4:14)

"Truly, truly, I say to you, whoever hears my word and believes him who sent me has eternal life. He does not come into judgment, but has passed from death to life. Truly, truly, I say to you, an hour is coming, and is now here, when the dead will hear the voice of the Son of God, and those who hear will live. For as the Father has life in himself, so he has granted the Son also to have life in himself. And he has given him authority to execute judgment, because he is the Son of Man." (John 5:24–27)

We receive this eternal life when we respond to the Gospel with faith. In that moment, the Spirit reconnects us with God. We receive the Holy Spirit, who takes up residence within us, and our spirit becomes one with His Spirit. We were disconnected from this kind of life; Jesus came to restore it to us. When this occurs, we are born again, from above.

This happened for me personally when I was five years old in the kitchen at home with my mom. She shared the Gospel with me, and we prayed together Jesus would forgive my sin and come to live inside my heart.

Remember our discussion about the Temple? The Temple had three main sections: the *Outer Court*, where any ceremonially clean person could come, the Holy Place, where the priests served according to God's instruction, and the *Most Holy Place*, where God's presence was manifestly present. These three places correspond with God's design for man. The *Outer Court* corresponds to our bodies. The *Holy Place* corresponds to our souls. The *Most Holy Place* corresponds to our spirits. In the New Covenant, we are each the Temple of the Holy Spirit. When He comes to indwell us, He takes up residence within the Most Holy Place.

"But he who is joined to the Lord becomes one spirit with him." (1 Corinthians 6:17)

"By which he has granted to us his precious and very great promises, so that through them you may become partakers of the divine nature, having escaped from the corruption that is in the world because of sinful desire." (2 Peter 1:4)

"Do you not know that you are God's temple and that God's Spirit dwells in you?" (1 Corinthians 3:16)

The Spirit Who Empowers

- **Ephesus**
  "And it happened that while Apollos was at Corinth, Paul passed through the inland country and came to Ephesus. There he found some disciples. And he said to them, 'Did you receive the Holy Spirit when you

believed?' And they said, 'No, we have not even heard that there is a Holy Spirit.' And he said, 'Into what then were you baptized? They said, 'Into John's baptism.' And Paul said, 'John baptized with the baptism of repentance, telling the people to believe in the one who was to come after him, that is, Jesus.' On hearing this, they were baptized in the name of the Lord Jesus. And when Paul had laid his hands on them, the Holy Spirit came on them, and they began speaking in tongues and prophesying. There were about twelve men in all." (Acts 19:1–7)

These men from Ephesus must have grown up in the same church I did. The Holy Spirit hadn't exactly been emphasized in their early discipleship experiences, for they didn't even know there was a Holy Spirit. I want us to take a close look at this passage, in light of what we've discussed in this chapter.

These men were disciples. These men were believers. These men had experienced a less than adequate water baptism. These men had not received the Holy Spirit.

The issue of water baptism is fairly straightforward. John's baptism anticipated the Messiah, but was inadequate as an expression of faith in Messiah. This was easily corrected with some simple teaching and an opportunity to be immersed in Jesus' name.

The issue of the Holy Spirit in this passage raises some

potential questions. Think of what we've already learned about the indwelling work of the Holy Spirit: a person receives the Holy Spirit when they first respond to the Gospel with faith. This is what it means to be born again. This is the nature of the new life in Christ we receive, and it is the inward life of the Spirit that constitutes regeneration. A deep connection with God by the Spirit is the very essence of the eternal life we receive when we first believe.

This being the case, Paul's question to the Ephesians is a bit confusing. If they are disciples—if they are believers—then they have already received the indwelling work of the Spirit. Theological ignorance of this reality would not make this any less true. They would simply need some good teaching to clarify, not an additional experience. Paul indicates that there is an experience of the Spirit, referred to here as *receiving the Holy Spirit*, which they might have received when they first believed; then again, they might not have—hence the question.

One might consider the possibility that although they are disciples, although they are believers, they are not yet disciples of and believers in Jesus. Perhaps they are disciples of John the Baptist. If they are disciples of and believers in something or someone besides Jesus, then this would explain why they haven't received the Holy Spirit. But, while explaining that issue, it would immediately create another one. For if this is their problem, then what they need to hear is the message about Jesus, and this isn't what Paul gave them.

It is clear from the text itself these men are disciples of and believers in Jesus. From this we can be confident they are born again, for that is how someone becomes born again. That they have experienced an inadequate water baptism is of no relevance, for regeneration occurs in response to faith and is followed by baptism. Water baptism is not a prerequisite for being born again.

Is Paul ignorant about all this? Is he unaware that receiving the Holy Spirit is the very thing that has made them disciples and is the very thing that certainly follows from having believed? I don't think so. If Paul is aware these men are believers—and he is—and if Paul is aware that, by definition, these believers have received the new life in Christ that comes through the indwelling work of the Spirit received by faith—and he is—then, when Paul asks these men if they received the Holy Spirit when they first believed, he must have had something else in mind beyond the Holy Spirit's indwelling work. The text really doesn't allow for another option.

If this were a unique instance then that might be one thing. But this is not a unique instance. Rather, this story simply highlights themes that run throughout Acts.

- **Jesus' Disciples**
Jesus' disciples received the indwelling work of the

Spirit in John 20.

> *"Jesus said to them again, 'Peace be with you. As the*
> *Father has sent me, even so I am sending you.' And*
> *when he had said this, he breathed on them and said*
> *to them, 'Receive the Holy Spirit.'"* (John 20:21–22)

This occurred immediately after His resurrection from the dead, on Sunday evening, about forty days prior to His ascension. The timeline is significant: the Holy Spirit's indwelling work was contingent upon Jesus' death and resurrection. The Holy Spirit *came upon* a very few people to empower them prior to Jesus' finished work.

The indwelling work of the Holy Spirit, however, is the very thing Jesus came to provide for us through His death and resurrection. It was necessary for Jesus to first complete His work before His followers could receive the Holy Spirit in this manner. Jesus quickly moved to impart the Holy Spirit during this initial post-resurrection appearance, and this demonstrates just how contingent upon Jesus' death and resurrection this indwelling work really is. Provision for sin had to be made before the life Adam lost for Mankind in the Garden of Eden could be restored.

Notice how Jesus imparted this to the disciples: He breathed on them. This imagery is biblically significant and clearly points back to Genesis 2.

"Then the Lord God formed the man of dust from the ground and breathed into his nostrils the breath of life, and the man became a living creature." (Genesis 2:7)

Jesus breathed and the disciples received the Holy Spirit. God breathed into Adam the breath of life. This clearly indicates what Jesus did was aimed at restoring the life of God through the indwelling presence of the Spirit lost in Genesis 3.

> *"The Holy Spirit indwells me to connect me to God. The Holy Spirit empowers me to help others connect to God."*

Jesus appeared at various times, in various ways, to a wide variety of people over a period of forty days prior to His ascension. Notice His final instructions to these same disciples almost six weeks later:

"And while staying with them he ordered them not to depart from Jerusalem, but to wait for the promise of the Father, which, he said, 'you heard from me; for

John baptized with water, but you will be baptized with the Holy Spirit not many days from now." (Acts 1:4–5)

He goes on to say:

"But you will receive power when the Holy Spirit has come upon you, and you will be my witnesses in Jerusalem and in all Judea and Samaria, and to the end of the earth." (Acts 1:8)

Jesus gives these instructions to men who have already received the Holy Spirit's indwelling work as recorded in John 20:22. Here, Jesus instructs them to wait in Jerusalem until they receive the Holy Spirit's empowering work.

When the Holy Spirit indwells us, He reconnects us with God as our source of life. He makes us new. When the Holy Spirit empowers us, He becomes our source of power to help others experience all God has provided for them. The Holy Spirit indwells me to connect me to God. The Holy Spirit empowers me to help others connect to God.

It is evident that the indwelling and empowering works of the Spirit are distinct, because they were received by the disciples subsequently, one after the other (Acts 1-2, 19). It must also be possible to experience both the indwelling and empowering works of the Spirit at the same time, because of the way Paul asked his question in Acts 19.

> *"And he said to them, 'Did you receive the Holy Spirit when you believed?' And they said, 'No, we have not even heard that there is a Holy Spirit.'"* (Acts 19:2)

The question itself implies they might have received the Holy Spirit in the manner to which he was referring when they first believed; but he recognizes they might not have.

- **Philip and the Samaritans**

Acts 8 recounts the story of Philip going to Samaria where he preached the gospel and performed many miracles.

> *"But when they believed Philip as he preached good news about the kingdom of God and the name of Jesus Christ, they were baptized, both men and women."* (Acts 8:12)

Note the sequence of events:

Philip preached the good news about the kingdom of God and the name of Jesus Christ.

They believed.

They were baptized.

Were these people born again? The clear and obvious

answer is *yes*. Did they receive the Holy Spirit? Yes, they had certainly received the indwelling work of the Spirit, for this is what it means to be born again and this experience is the definite result of faith in Christ. Look at what happens after this:

"Now when the apostles at Jerusalem heard that Samaria had received the word of God, they sent to them Peter and John, who came down and prayed for them that they might receive the Holy Spirit, for he had not yet fallen on any of them, but they had only been baptized in the name of the Lord Jesus." (Acts 8:14–16)

Though they were believers, the Holy Spirit *had not yet fallen on any of them*. In saying *they had only been baptized in the name of the Lord Jesus,* the strong implication is that another baptism was needed— a baptism that could be described in terms of the Holy Spirit falling upon them. This is precisely what had happened to Jesus' disciples in Acts 2, the very experience Jesus described as *The Baptism in the Holy Spirit* in Acts 1.

"When the day of Pentecost arrived, they were all together in one place. And suddenly there came from heaven a sound like a mighty rushing wind, and it

filled the entire house where they were sitting. And divided tongues as of fire appeared to them and rested on each one of them. And they were all filled with the Holy Spirit and began to speak in other tongues as the Spirit gave them utterance." (Acts 2:1–4)

"For John baptized with water, but you will be baptized with the Holy Spirit not many days from now." (Acts 1:5)

Look at the result when Peter and John prayed for these Samaritan disciples to receive the Holy Spirit, who had not yet come upon them.

"Then they laid their hands on them and they received the Holy Spirit." (Acts 8:17)

This is similar to the Ephesian experience, evident when both passages are compared.

"And when Paul had laid his hands on them, the Holy Spirit came on them, and they began speaking in tongues and prophesying." (Acts 19:6)

With the Samaritans in Acts 8, nothing is mentioned about either tongues or prophecy. Something observable occurred, for Simon desired to purchase this ability to lay hands on people and bring them into this experience. Was it tongues? Prophecy? We simply don't know, but something got Simon's attention. Whatever he witnessed was imparted through the laying on of hands, and described as the Holy Spirit *coming upon* them, and described in terms of *receiving the Holy Spirit.*

> *"Even Simon himself believed, and after being baptized he continued with Philip. And seeing signs and great miracles performed, he was amazed."* (Acts 8:13)

> *"Then they laid their hands on them and they received the Holy Spirit. Now when Simon saw that the Spirit was given through the laying on of the apostles' hands, he offered them money, saying, 'Give me this power also, so that anyone on whom I lay my hands may receive the Holy Spirit.'"* (Acts 8:17–19)

- **Cornelius' House**

Acts 10 relates a wonderful story about Peter and Cornelius. Cornelius was a Gentile, and Peter, of course, a nice Jewish boy. God gave Peter a vision in which he was asked to eat lots of unclean foods Jews were forbidden to eat. This vision was a metaphor, directing Peter to be open to taking the Gospel to the Gentiles. Peter went to Cornelius' house in obedience to God, and preached the good news about Jesus.

> *"While Peter was still saying these things, the Holy Spirit fell on all who heard the word. And the believers from among the circumcised who had come with Peter were amazed, because the gift of the Holy Spirit was poured out even on the Gentiles. For they were hearing them speaking in tongues and extolling God. Then Peter declared, 'Can anyone withhold water for baptizing these people, who have received the Holy Spirit just as we have?' And he commanded them to be baptized in the name of Jesus Christ. Then they asked him to remain for some days."* (Acts 10:44–48)

Leave it to God to make sure this story is included in scripture. God seems very interested in ensuring we don't get formulaic about any of this. The normal sequence, it seems, should be:

1. Believe the gospel and receive the indwelling work of the Spirit.

2. Get baptized in water.

3. Receive the empowering work of the Spirit who *comes upon* and *fills.*

In the middle of his message, somewhere around the third point or the poem, Cornelius, along with his entire household begins to speak in tongues—while Peter was still preaching! This is an obvious example of when both the indwelling and empowering works of the Spirit are received and experienced simultaneously. Though they are distinct works of the Spirit, they can be experienced concurrently. There can be no argument against baptizing these Gentiles in water once this has happened.

It seems clear there are two distinct works of the Holy Spirit in the life of the believer. Believers receive the indwelling work of the Spirit when they respond to the gospel with faith, reconnecting them with God and eternal life. Believers may also receive the empowering work of the Spirit when the Holy Spirit comes upon them and fills them. This is distinct from the indwelling of the Spirit, though it may be received concurrently. The empowering work of the Spirit is about boldness in sharing the gospel, and power to help others experience God.

10

Faith

Better Get Ready!
We have three children. My wife delivered each of them at home with the help of a midwife. My wife is the coolest woman on the planet.

Home birth was Nancy's idea, not mine; I must admit I took a bit of convincing to warm up to the idea. No doctors? No drugs? What if something goes wrong? Nancy's take—hospitals are for sick people and pregnancy is not a sickness. I got used to the idea. Eventually.

Pregnancy usually lasts forty weeks, but it's normally safe for a baby to be born any time after about the thirty-sixth week. Our first child was due during the first week of January, and on Monday of the thirty-eighth week, God and I had a little conversation. This was Monday, December 18. My birthday is December 22.

"God, wanna know what I want for my birthday present this year?"

Sure, God said in reply, as if eager to find out. He knows everything. We both are aware of this, but He humors me sometimes. Often, really.

"I want the baby to be born on my birthday." I had to go with *the baby* because we were waiting until delivery to find out gender and then settle on a name.

His response? *Ok.*

I then filled Nancy in on the details about my conversation with God, letting her know she should expect the baby on Friday. She appeared bewildered and somewhat unconvinced. What I didn't know was she had planned a rather large surprise party for my birthday on Friday. My conversation with God, if genuine, represented quite an interruption to her plans. She couldn't tell me this, because if I somehow hadn't heard God as accurately as claimed, she still wanted to protect the surprise.

She replied, "But I'm not ready yet."

Having a baby at home requires a good bit of preparation. The house has to be prepped. There is gear to buy, supplies to order. In the movies, you just need hot water and towels. This is a myth. She wasn't ready.

"Well, then," I said, "You'd better get ready. The baby's coming on Friday."

I called Susan, our midwife, to give her a heads-up about Friday so she could keep her schedule clear. She thought I was very cute.

Lauren Elizabeth Smith was born at 10:14 pm on Friday, December 22.

Hearing God speak, believing what He has said, and declaring what He's said with your own mouth—this is the essence of how faith works. Faith is, however, widely misunderstood and misrepresented.

> *"Through faith, the heavenly reality of God's Kingdom breaks into my present view."*

What is Faith?

"Now faith is the substance of things hoped for, the evidence of things not seen." (Hebrews 11:1, NKJV)

We've spent quite a bit of time exploring God's desire to help us live *now* from the perspective of *then,* and *here* from the perspective of *there.* This definition of faith from the writer of Hebrews fits snugly into that framework.

What is hoped for is what is *then,* rather than *now.*

What is unseen is *there,* rather than *here.*

Faith is the means by which I can experience *here* and *now* what is *there* and *then.* Through faith, the future reality of the age to come breaks into my present experience. Through faith, the heavenly reality of God's Kingdom breaks into my present view.

Faith is belief, in that it agrees with God's revealed word. Faith is trust, in that it relies upon God's revealed character. The meaning of faith in Hebrews 11:1 includes these ideas of belief and trust, but takes us beyond both into something much more concrete.

Faith is substance—the substance of things hoped for. The Greek word for substance refers to the reality of a thing, its essence. Faith is not merely a sign that points toward a heavenly reality, faith is the substance of that reality. Faith is the present substance, the reality, and the essence of what is anticipated in the future. Faith is the means whereby the future reality becomes my present reality.

Not only is faith the presently experienced reality of what we hope for, faith is also the evidence of what we do not see. Faith is evidence. The ESV says *the conviction of things not seen.* Evidence. Conviction. A charge has been made. Evidence has been viewed. The court is fully persuaded. The conclusion is certain.

Evidence.

There is a heavenly reality we cannot see with our natural eyes, but faith works *here* to give us access to *there.* When we have faith, we have concrete certainty and total persuasion of a reality we cannot yet see in the natural, a heavenly reality that must be seen and experienced by faith before it can be manifested on earth.

What is faith? Faith is belief and trust—it's both of

those things. But what kind of belief? What kind of trust? Faith is not a blind leap into the abstract. Faith is the kind of belief and trust that works in the present to lay hold of a future reality. Faith is the kind of belief and trust that works from an earthly perspective to lay hold of a heavenly reality. Faith is a way of seeing, a way of accessing, a way of gripping, a way of pulling heavenly reality into the earthly realm, and a way of pulling New Creation reality into the present. Faith is a firm grip on a concrete reality that is both heavenly and of the age to come.

When faith sees, when faith accesses, when faith grabs hold, old things pass away and new things come—New Creation.

What Faith Understands

"By faith we understand that the worlds were framed by the word of God, so that the things which are seen were not made of things which are visible." (Hebrews 11:3, NKJV)

Because faith sees *here* from the perspective of *there*, and *now* from the perspective of *then*, faith sees natural reality in a supernatural way. Faith comprehends the non-material origin of the material world. The children's cartoon *Scooby Doo* taught us to see the natural explanation behind every event appearing to be supernatural. In each episode, the goblins, ghosts, or monsters turn out to be the creepy and villainous neighbor next door—*who would have gotten away with it too if it weren't for those meddling kids.* There's always a natural explanation for everything.

In contrast, faith teaches us to see the spiritual origin underneath what initially appears to be natural. If material reality originates from and is sustained by God's word, then material reality is, at its root, spiritual. Creation *ex nihilo* means God created everything from nothing; this is the very definition of supernatural. And if all of nature is supernatural, then the distinction between the two categories vanishes.

There is no natural and supernatural. There is only God, and that which God has made. All of physical reality is derived from what is non-material. All that is seen is made from what is unseen.

The implications of this verse are staggering. If I want to live a life of faith, then I must embrace a different way of seeing reality. The lenses handed to me by modernism and the Enlightenment will only distort my view of reality, working against the life of faith. Modern man sees only the seen, denying the unseen. When modern man acknowledges the unseen, he relegates it to a category completely distinct from the seen: the unseen is where we go when we die, the unseen is another kind of place altogether. Material existence functions independently of the unseen realm, working exclusively by natural cause and effect.

Faith presents an alternate view. As we've discussed previously, option one is *materialism*—matter is all that is. Option two is a kind of *dualism*—matter and spirit both exist, but independently, distinct from one another. Option three is matter and spirit are deeply integrated, the seen with the unseen. This is the way faith sees. This is what faith understands.

A central theme of scripture is that it describes created reality, whether material or not, as both originating from and being sustained by God, through the word of God—which is both unseen and non-material.

> *"For by Him all things were created that are in heaven and that are on earth, visible and invisible, whether thrones or dominions or principalities or powers. All things were created through Him and for Him. And He is before all things, and in Him all things consist."* (Colossians 1:16–17, NKJV)

These verses intentionally group all things together as having the same origin, heaven and earth, visible and invisible. As we discussed in Chapter 6, all things have a non-material, spiritual origin: Jesus. Since the incarnation and resurrection, Jesus is now material too—which only strengthens the point.

> *"Yet for us there is one God, the Father, from whom are all things and for whom we exist, and one Lord, Jesus Christ, through whom are all things and through whom we exist."* (1 Corinthians 8:6)

Twice, this verse speaks of *all things.* This must include all created things, whether material or spiritual, whether earthly or heavenly. And what does this verse tell us about all things? All things are both *from* and *for* God, and all things are *through* God. The existence of everything is rooted in God. God sustains the existence of everything. The purpose of all existence is God. There is no such thing as material existence distinct from spiritual reality. There is no such thing as *natural,* if by that we mean what is not supernatural.

> *"In the beginning was the Word, and the Word was with God, and the Word was God. He was in the beginning with God. All things were made through him, and without him was not any thing made that was made."* (John 1:1–3)

Here we have the clearest possible statement regarding the origin of material reality. Where does the natural world find its origin? In the Word of God, the Word who is God. Creation wasn't, and then it was. What produced this result? God spoke His Word. This is not natural; it is supernatural. It is matter, but it is not merely material. All that is material is spiritual in its origin, at its root. In verse 14 of the same chapter, we see this Word became flesh. The spiritual became material. This is the essence of all of Creation and this is the essence of God's plan for New Creation.

> "*Who being the brightness of His glory and the express image of His person, and upholding all things by the word of His power, when He had by Himself purged our sins, sat down at the right hand of the Majesty on high.*" (Hebrews 1:3, NKJV)

Not only does created material reality have its origin in the Word of God, which is non-material, this same Word also presently sustains it.

This way of understanding reality is completely counter-cultural, counter-intuitive for modern western thinkers. But this is what faith understands. This is what faith sees. Many of us, recognizing a need for greater faith, try to bear down and believe more and trust more. When this doesn't produce the desired result, we try even harder to believe and trust. But this is not the solution.

Lack of faith is often simply a wrong perspective: we see reality in the wrong way. We see the material as distinct from the spiritual. To see the material realm as independent of the spiritual realm will absolutely stand in the way of our calling to be conduits through which God's kingdom comes and earth is influenced by heaven. It's impossible to believe for *on earth as in heaven* if we fail to understand the fundamental way these two realities are integrated.

What Faith Believes

"And without faith it is impossible to please him, for whoever would draw near to God must believe that he exists and that he rewards those who seek him." (Hebrews 11:6)

In this verse there are two parallel contingencies: first a negative, then a positive. A *contingency* exists when an outcome is uncertain, dependent upon whether or not the needed *cause* occurs. For instance, I might get up early in the morning tomorrow to write, if I can first manage to get to bed tonight at a reasonable hour. For me, getting up early tomorrow is contingent upon going to bed early tonight. If x, then y. If not x, then not y.

The first contingency in this verse is stated negatively, and has to do with faith and pleasing God. If I don't have faith, I won't please God. If not x, then not y. The reverse is implied: if I do have faith, I will please God. If x, then y.

The second contingency is stated positively. The order is also reversed, with the cause stated after the consequence. I will draw near to God if I believe He is good and a rewarder. *Y*, if *x*. I will draw near to God if I believe God exists and will reward me when I seek Him. Again, the reverse is implied. I won't draw near to God if I don't believe God exists, or that He rewards those who seek Him.

Statement One:
Without faith, I will not please God.
If not *x*, then not *y*.

Statement Two:
I will come to God if I believe He is good and a rewarder.
Y, if *x*.

In both statements, the issue of faith is present. Faith is the cause upon which the outcome is contingent. In the first statement, the outcome is pleasing God. In the second, the outcome is drawing near to God. In both statements, the necessary cause that will produce the outcome is faith.

Taken together, these two statements tell us something very important about God's character. What pleases God? At first glance, it might appear faith is what pleases God, but this isn't what it means.

Drawing near to God—that's what pleases Him. If I have faith, I will draw near to God. In the first statement, faith is the condition required to produce the outcome of pleasing God. In the second statement, faith is the necessary condition required to produce the outcome of drawing near to God.

Faith is necessary for me to please God by approaching Him—faith that grasps not just God's existence, but also His character as a rewarder of those who seek Him.

"Let us then with confidence draw near to the throne of grace, that we may receive mercy and find grace to help in time of need." (Hebrews 4:16)

"For through him we both have access in one Spirit to the Father." (Ephesians 2:18)

"This was according to the eternal purpose that he has realized in Christ Jesus our Lord, in whom we have boldness and access with confidence through our faith in him." (Ephesians 3:11–12)

"Let us draw near with a true heart in full assurance of faith, with our hearts sprinkled clean from an evil conscience and our bodies washed with pure water." (Hebrews 10:22)

"Draw near to God, and he will draw near to you." (James 4:8a)

The stated goal of Hebrews 11:6 is that we please God by drawing near to Him. We can and will only do this if we have faith. Specifically, we need the kind of faith that understands something about God's nature. God exists. (Well, of course! I'm not likely to draw near to God if I don't believe He exists.) This is first, necessary, and quite obvious.

But I must also accurately see God's character. It is not enough to believe God exists. What do I believe to be true about this God who exists? What is the content of my faith? Do I believe He is good? If not, I will not draw near; if so, I will. My belief that God is good and responsive (*a rewarder of those who seek Him*) is not what pleases God. It pleases God when I draw near to Him, but I will not draw near if I don't believe He is good and responsive.

We have taken a close look at what faith understands, what faith believes, and what this produces. Faith understands something very important about Creation and faith believes something very important about the Creator. When I understand that what is seen is rooted in the unseen, and I believe God is good and responsive, I will please God by drawing near. At the same time, I will become a conduit through which God's good and responsive nature is reflected from heaven to earth.

Abraham's Example

"What then shall we say was gained by Abraham, our forefather according to the flesh? For if Abraham was justified by works, he has something to boast about, but not before God. For what does the Scripture say? 'Abraham believed God, and it was counted to him as righteousness.'" (Romans 4:1–3)

The main point of this entire passage is that Abraham was justified on the basis of faith rather than works, but my purpose is to ask another question of the text: What did Abraham believe? What was the content of his faith? There are several key verses:

"For the promise to Abraham and his offspring that he would be heir of the world did not come through the law but through the righteousness of faith." (Romans 4:13)

"As it is written, 'I have made you the father of many

"Abraham was justified by believing, not by obeying."

nations'—in the presence of the God in whom he believed, who gives life to the dead and calls into existence the things that do not exist. In hope he believed against hope, that he should become the father of many nations, as he had been told, 'So shall your offspring be.'" (Romans 4:17–18)

"Fully convinced that God was able to do what he had promised." (Romans 4:21)

The aim of this section of Paul's letter is to demonstrate that justification is received on the basis of faith rather than works. Abraham was justified by believing, not by obeying. Others will be justified only if they share his faith.

Paul's point isn't that because Abraham believed in justification by faith, we should as well. Paul's point is to convince us of a doctrinal reality, but not by demonstrating that Abraham believed in this doctrine. Abraham's faith wasn't in justification by faith; Abraham's faith was his belief God would do the miraculous, just as He had promised.

The verses listed above make this very clear. Verse 13 tells us what Abraham believed was God's promise that his descendants would be heirs of the world. Abraham believed God for a miracle, since he had no children—he and Sarah were unable to conceive. In effect, by believing

God's promise, Abraham believed God for a miracle of healing! It was faith in God for the miraculous that served as the basis of Abraham's justification. God promised a miracle. Abraham believed God's promise and this faith was credited to him as righteousness.

What was the specific content of Abraham's faith? He believed God would enable them to conceive. He believed God would greatly bless his offspring. He believed God gives life to the dead. He believed God calls those things into existence that do not exist. He believed God is able.

Let's connect the dots between Abraham's example of faith and what we learned about faith from Hebrews 11. Faith allows me to lay hold now of a future reality that is not yet, and a heavenly reality that is not here. Additionally, faith has a certain way of perceiving created reality, recognizing the supernatural in all that is natural, knowing God has called all things into existence by speaking, making the visible from the invisible. Faith is the necessary condition for drawing near to God, thus pleasing God, because faith rightly understands God is good and responsive to those who seek Him. Can we observe these truths in Abraham's example of faith?

The promise that Abraham's children would inherit the earth is certainly the declaration of a future reality, something not yet. The promise that Abraham and Sarah would be enabled to conceive a child is something that, at that time, was heavenly (God had declared it) and not earthly (they were barren). Abraham realized God's nature is to call things into existence that don't currently exist. This is the nature of created reality that faith understands, and Abraham clearly perceived it. Finally, Abraham perceived God's goodness and responsiveness, for he trusted God would keep His promises.

Not Faith in Faith

Abraham was not justified because he believed in his own faith. He was justified because he believed God's promise. This raises a very important issue that merits clarification.

In looking at Hebrews 11:6, we noted that faith is not what pleases God—drawing near to God pleases God. Faith is not the cause; it's the necessary condition. Many believers, however, tend to mistake faith as a cause.

Think of a sailboat for a moment. Wind is the *cause* of the sailboat's movement, but not without the sail. The sail alone is powerless to generate anything; it can only capture the power of the wind. It is important to understand the distinction between a *cause* and a *condition*. When I mistakenly think of faith as a *cause* rather than a necessary *condition*, I will always risk falling into the trap of believing in faith. Faith in faith is not the answer, no more than a sail can harness its own strength.

We must understand what makes faith strong—faith's object makes faith strong. What faith is aimed at determines faith's effectiveness. The one believed in determines the power of belief. I may need more sail, but only so I can capture more wind. Only wind moves the boat. The sail is only as effective as the wind it captures. When I mistake the sail for the wind, faith for the object of faith, I position myself for great frustration. I must trust in God, not in my ability to trust in God. Faith in faith is ultimately an expression of faith in self.

If faith is a cause, then the strength of faith should be measured by its sincerity and fervency—the more sincere and fervent my faith, the greater my faith, right? But what if this isn't true?

Consider this example. Scripture teaches that Jesus is the exclusive way to be reconciled to God. When I have faith in Christ, God's provision of salvation through Christ is activated in my life. What makes this effective? Is it the sincerity and fervency of my faith? Or is it the sufficiency of what God has provided for me through Christ? What if I had sincere and fervent faith in another god, another savior, rather than in Christ? Then my faith would be futile, for it would be wrongly aimed. My faith in Jesus is strong, not because my faith is strong, but because Jesus is strong. Even a little faith—faith the size of a mustard seed—rightly aimed at Jesus, is strong faith.

So many are constantly trying hard to believe more, recognizing a need for greater faith. But if I want my faith to increase, I shouldn't focus on trying harder to believe, but rather upon more fully perceiving who God is and what He has done. As I step into a deeper revelation of God as a rewarder of those who seek Him, I will draw closer to Him. The revelation of who God is comes first; faith will follow revelation.

> "So faith comes from hearing, and hearing through the word of Christ." (Romans 10:17)

Deeper revelation enables me to aim my faith more fully at who God actually is, thus making faith stronger. Stronger faith will prompt me to draw even closer to God, which will then lead to deeper revelation. Deeper revelation will produce stronger faith; on and on it goes. But throughout the process, my focus is not on growing my faith. My focus is upon seeing God more clearly and drawing closer to Him.

Focusing on Jesus is the key.

11

Abiding

"I am the vine; you are the branches. Whoever abides in me and I in him, he it is that bears much fruit, for apart from me you can do nothing." (John 15:5)

The Vineyard

Michael and Travis were high school students in the small youth group I was pastoring. During one particular season, I had the opportunity to spend some time with these guys talking about God, life, and the Bible. We went fishing a few times. We hung out at my house. There was a burger joint on the town square that smothered their burgers with loads of grated sharp cheddar. We went there a few times, too.

One Saturday morning, we met early, climbed in Travis' red Chevy pickup truck, and drove about 45 minutes to

Grapevine, Texas. Neither Michael nor Travis had a clue where we were going or why; I just gave directions along the way. When we pulled into the parking lot for a local vineyard, they both looked a bit confused.

I had permission from the manager to take these guys out onto the property, so we walked right out into the middle of the field. It's not a large vineyard, about ten acres. Though right up against a fairly busy state highway, they've managed to maintain a very serene and old world feel to the place. The grapevines are planted uniformly in neat rows, wide enough to provide easy walking space. The vines themselves shoot up from the ground, twisting and turning their way up long, thin stabilizing poles, branches and leaves growing out in every direction.

We arrived in the planned spot just as the sun had made its full appearance above the horizon. There wasn't any traffic. It was very quiet. Michael and Travis turned to look at me, their expressions clearly stating *What now?*

"Listen," I said.

They waited. They listened. They didn't hear anything. They were obviously confused. Travis had this way of cocking one eyebrow high on his forehead.

"Just listen."

They tried. They were both pretty good sports about the whole thing, really. Both of them adopted very intent, focused expressions, squinting their eyes and tucking their chins down toward their chest just a bit as they attempted to follow my bewildering instruction.

There was nothing to hear.

This was my point.

But there was something to see. Spread throughout the branches of each vine, sometimes hiding underneath the deeply green foliage, sometimes immediately visible with just a quick glance, were lots and lots of small grapes. Nothing mature, nothing ready for harvest, but the fruit was there. Growing.

> *"But God is good. He prunes us to allow increased fruitfulness."*

And there was no sound. No deep sighs of frustration. No cries of labored difficulty. No groans of strain. The branches were making no sounds whatsoever. It's like they weren't even working. They seemed completely at rest. All they had to do to produce fruit was stay connected to the vine.

Abide.

Abiding and Faith

The word *faith* doesn't appear in the passage, but John 15:1-11 may well be the best passage about faith in the Bible. We're going to take the time to explore some of its themes section by section.

"I am the true vine, and my Father is the vinedresser. Every branch in me that does not bear fruit he takes away, and every branch that does bear fruit he prunes, that it may bear more fruit." (John 15:1–2)

God thinks like a farmer: His goal is fruitfulness, and His activity is aimed toward that end. He doesn't hurry. He prepares the soil, plants the seed, tends to weeds, provides water, and takes care of harmful bugs. He waits patiently. He harvests the fruit. He prunes. Oh, does He prune!

Pruning occurs when the farmer takes shears and begins to strategically cut back a plant's superfluous growth to facilitate increased fruitfulness. I wonder if many choose not to abide simply because the pruning process in their life is too difficult, too painful. Believing in God's goodness, the last thing they anticipated was Him coming at them with a sharp object and beginning to cut away parts of their lives. So they withdraw. They pull back to avoid being cut back. But God is good. He prunes us to allow increased fruitfulness. He cuts us back so we can grow more, and in the right ways. The entire passage is about abiding, about staying connected to the vine. This is not compulsory; it requires our surrender. We must yield.

Abiding is optional. Only abiding produces fruitfulness. If I choose not to abide, I will not bear fruit. If, as a branch, I don't bear fruit, Jesus says the farmer will take me away. Fruitfulness is not optional. Jesus elaborates on this in verse six:

> "If anyone does not abide in me he is thrown away like a branch and withers; and the branches are gathered, thrown into the fire, and burned." (John 15:6)

Sounds pretty serious, doesn't it? Fruitfulness matters. Only abiding produces fruitfulness.

> "Already you are clean because of the word that I have spoken to you." (John 15:3)

At first glance, verse three may seem disconnected from the previous two verses. Notice, however, the connection between *clean* in verse three and *prunes* in verse two. Both words come from the same root; *clean* is simply the adjective version of the verb *prunes*. Once you are pruned, you are clean.

In this verse, Jesus is letting us know how pruning occurs: it is His word that prunes us. It is the process of hearing God's voice and experiencing the resulting transformation as we align with what He says—and obey—that produces pruning. In this verse, Jesus is telling this group of disciples they've already experienced some of this pruning.

Abiding produces fruitfulness. Fruitfulness prompts pruning to increase fruitfulness. The Father's method for pruning in our lives is the voice of Jesus. Who does God speak to? Those who are fruitful. Who are fruitful? Those who abide. In Jesus' farming metaphor, abiding refers to the life-giving connection between the branch and the vine, whereby the branch looks to the vine as its source and remains connected to the vine. This illustrates for us what God desires, that we would stay connected to His presence, looking to Him alone as our source.

Sometimes, in seasons where we are struggling to hear God's voice, the issue is ultimately that we are not looking to God as our source, not staying deeply connected to His presence. Remember Hebrews 11:6? What pleases God is when I come to Him. Connection. Nearness. When I come to Him, the resulting nearness and connection will produce fruitfulness. Intimacy produces fruitfulness. We see this in the natural (think babies), and it is also true of our relationship with Christ.

Fruitfulness will prompt pruning. God prunes us by speaking to us. He uses His word to cut away the superfluous in our lives to make us more fruitful, making the life we receive more focused and better aimed. His Word is sharper than a double-edged sword.

"Abide in me, and I in you. As the branch cannot bear fruit by itself, unless it abides in the vine, neither can

you, unless you abide in me. I am the vine; you are the branches. Whoever abides in me and I in him, he it is that bears much fruit, for apart from me you can do nothing." (John 15:4–5)

In verses four and five, Jesus gives further expression to this same point, contrasting our two main source options. One option is to be our own source, looking to produce fruit based upon our own abilities and resources. This is the condition of fallen Man—self as source. When I am looking to produce my own significance, provision, or identity through what I know, what I can do, or what response I can manipulate from others, then I am like a branch disconnected from the vine. I will wither, die, and ultimately be discarded. Jesus is giving us a clear description of the exact state of sinful man and the precise dilemma for which He is the solution. Apart from Him, I can do nothing. He is my source; there is no other available.

God's solution to my problem is to become my source, to enable me to connect deeply to Him and receive from Him all I need. When observing a grapevine, it is sometimes difficult to tell where the vine ends and the branches begin. There is oneness present, an organic explosion of twisting and turning within and around, between vine, branch, and other branches. The branches are in the vine and the vine in the branches, each point of life-giving connection a merging of existence and an overlap of substance. *Abide in me, and I in you.* This is the kind of life Jesus came to bring us into. It is a life of connection, a life of pruning, and a life of fruitfulness. It is a life focused upon His presence, a life responsive to His voice, and a life of deep abiding joy.

"If you abide in me, and my words abide in you, ask whatever you wish, and it will be done for you. By this my Father is glorified, that you bear much fruit and so prove to be my disciples. As the Father has loved me, so have I loved you. Abide in my love. If you keep my commandments, you will abide in my love, just as I have kept my Father's commandments and abide in his love. These things I have spoken to you, that my joy may be in you, and that your joy may be full." (John 15:7–11)

Much appears to hinge upon answered prayer. In this section, Jesus gives definition to what He means by fruitfulness. *Ask whatever you wish, and it will be done for you* is the *by this* that brings glory to the Father; it is equated to bearing *much fruit,* and serves to prove we are actually Christ's disciples. It is the product of being in Christ and of Christ being in us. The fruitfulness of answered prayer is the result of this intimate, life-giving connection.

However, *ask whatever you wish* is not a blank check. It

is limited by the context. Abiding in Christ and allowing Jesus' words to abide in us will shape our desires, and will therefore ultimately shape what we ask. When what we ask for has been formed through abiding, then we will receive whatever we ask. If answered prayer does not characterize our lives, this should be a cause for concern. Either we are not asking, or what we are asking for is not a product of abiding. Without this evidence, is there really any proof we are connected to Christ at all?

This is not to say every single prayer we pray must be answered in order to have confidence in our connection to Christ. But every prayer we pray that is shaped by our connection to Christ will be answered. Remember the pruning? When we are a little fruitful, the Father prunes us in order that we might be even more fruitful. If we define fruitfulness as answered prayer, then our expectation should be: some fruit, followed by pruning, followed by increased fruit, followed by more pruning, and so on. This is what proves we as branches are connected to the vine. This is what proves the Father is our gardener.

Jesus then says if we keep His commandments like He has kept the Father's commandments, we will abide in His love just like He abides in the Father's love. This could appear to

"Our best efforts to obey the commandments will not even get us in the door."

be an endorsement of legalism and performance-based relationship. Through that lens, we might paraphrase this verse as if Jesus said *If you obey the rules as well as me, then the Father and I will love you.* Can this possibly be what Jesus is saying? If so, it flies in the face of most everything else He ever said. It all depends upon what Jesus means when He speaks of His commandments and obedience.

Let's take a look at a key verse from the Sermon on the Mount.

> *"Do not think that I came to destroy the Law or the Prophets. I did not come to destroy but to fulfill. For assuredly, I say to you, till heaven and earth pass away, one jot or one tittle will by no means pass from the law till all is fulfilled. Whoever therefore breaks one of the least of these commandments, and teaches men so, shall be called least in the kingdom of heaven; but whoever does and teaches them, he shall be called great in the kingdom of heaven. For I say to you, that unless your righteousness exceeds the righteousness of the scribes and Pharisees, you will by no means enter the kingdom of heaven." (Matthew 5:17–20, NKJV)*

Jesus came to fulfill the Law. In this passage, Jesus very clearly affirms the significance of the Law, every commandment within the Law, and the importance of keeping the Law and teaching others to do the same. Jesus, along with Paul, consistently demonstrates that if there's a problem, it's not with the Law. The problem is with humans.

The key is in verse twenty. Our righteousness must be greater than the Pharisees' righteousness—a high bar. No group of people, perhaps in all of history, has been as diligent in their efforts to keep the Law as the Pharisees. According to Jesus, this is insufficient. Our best efforts to obey the commandments will not even get us in the door.

In the following verses, Jesus begins to address specific issues like anger, lust, divorce, vows, and vengeance. In each case, Jesus uses the phrases *You have heard it said,* followed by *but I say to you.* It might appear Jesus has come, not to abolish the Law, but rather to ramp it up a notch, to make the impossible even more impossible. No longer is the standard *don't murder.* Now the standard is *don't even be angry.*

Jesus is not simply escalating what the Law requires—He is inviting us to be transformed, to be made new. The kind of righteousness He offers, the kind that exceeds anyone else's righteousness, is not based on our performance at all; it's based on His. This righteousness is extended to us through God's powerful grace, a grace that works within us to transform our very nature.[1] The grace-given righteousness Jesus offers can turn a person into someone completely new, with a new nature and brand new motivations and thought processes.[2] Jesus isn't challenging us to try harder to follow an escalated version of the Old Testament legal system. Recognizing the futility of human effort, Jesus is offering complete transformation.

In light of this, how should we view these verses about obedience and the commandments in John 15? What kind of obedience is Jesus talking about? What are *His* commandments? The entire context is addressing the issue of fruitfulness produced through intimate, life-giving connection with Him. Make no mistake about it; obedience to Jesus is an essential and significant part of our discipleship. But this is not an obedience rooted in self-effort. This is an obedience rooted in sharing the nature of Christ as our source.[3] This is obedience responsive to God's presence and voice. This is an obedience that flows from perfect love. This is an obedience that surges with fullness of joy.

What does any of this have to do with faith?

Everything.

Without faith, we would never connect; we would never abide. Faith is the conduit through which we receive from God. If we define fruitfulness in terms of answered prayer, then faith is essential. This entire passage is all about faith, without focusing on faith at all, and this is the point.

Faith is essential, but it should never be our focus.

Faith will grow and function; not as we focus upon faith, but as we focus upon connecting more deeply with God, receiving all He has for us as our source of life, abiding in His presence, and responding to His voice. Faith is not about my effort to believe, it is about my surrender as a branch to the vine.

Faith abides. Faith receives. Faith rests.

Rest

"So then, there remains a Sabbath rest for the people of God, for whoever has entered God's rest has also rested from his works as God did from his." (Hebrews 4:9–10)

The writer of Hebrews uses the word *rest* to pack up a lot of important ideas. The concept of Sabbath goes all the way back to Genesis 1, where God rested after finishing His work in Creation. In the New Testament, Sabbath carries this same idea: in Christ, God has finished His work of redemption, providing all that is needed for New Creation. When we enter into God's rest, we fully rely upon Christ's finished work.

The first *rest* in these verses is connected to Sabbath. The two English words *Sabbath rest* are used to translate the single Greek word *sabbatismos*. This is an excellent translation, because we might tend to think of Sabbath merely as a day of the week, when the Hebrew term actually comes from a root that means *to cease, or to rest.* The second *rested* in verse ten is from the Greek word *katapausis,* which literally means *to make something cease.* It's used outside of this passage only in Acts 14, where it is translated *restrained.*

> *"Even with these words they scarcely restrained the people from offering sacrifice to them." (Acts 14:18)*

This makes the idea very clear. The people in Acts 14 were in the process of offering sacrifices, but were restrained from doing so. They were doing something, and were made to quit doing it. The term refers to the cessation of activity or effort. In Hebrews 4:10, a category of people is described who have ceased working; they have stopped doing their own works. They have *entered God's rest.* This *rest* is slightly different, referring not only to the act of ceasing labor, but also to the place of rest, a dwelling place.

> *"Heaven is my throne, and the earth is my footstool. What kind of house will you build for me, says the Lord, or what is the place of my rest?" (Acts 7:49)*

The place of rest carries both the connotation of God's presence as well as the inheritance of God's people. It is

God's place of rest. It's also theirs.

The next verse might initially appear contradictory:

"Let us therefore strive to enter that rest, so that no one may fall by the same sort of disobedience." (Hebrews 4:11)

In English, *strive* can indicate labor. Are we being instructed to work to stop working? The word actually speaks of earnestness, eagerness. The writer is telling us to be eager to enter into God's place of rest. Israel, after the negative report from the ten spies, wasn't eager to enter the Promised Land, God's place of rest. In contrast, we are encouraged to eagerly desire to enter into God's dwelling place, the place where God has ceased from His works—and the place where we cease from our own. Israel didn't want to enter in because they were afraid of the giants. The place of rest looked like a lot of pain and difficulty to them. When we take a look at what's in store for us as we enter in, we might feel the same way.

"For the word of God is living and active, sharper than any two-edged sword, piercing to the division of soul and of spirit, of joints and of marrow, and discerning the thoughts and intentions of the heart. And no creature is hidden from his sight, but all are naked and exposed to the eyes of him to whom we must give

account." (Hebrews 4:12–13)

Jesus, the High Priest, wields a sword.[4] His words cut. They pierce. They divide. They expose. Israel didn't want to face the giants' size and swords. How often do we fail to draw near because we know God's word will not allow us to remain hidden and opaque before God? The term *exposed* is a sacrificial term, a very graphic word picture describing the act of bending back the head to expose the neck. Israel had the opportunity to enter the place of God's rest but refused in order to avoid the giants. How often do we fail to draw near to God because of shame?

God is calling us to a life of rest. It's the kind of life where you don't have to hide anymore. No more laboring to be good enough, to perform. God calls us to cease from our own efforts. But this is not a passive rest, a place of boredom and inactivity. This is the kind of rest that chooses to climb upon the altar before the High Priest. This is the kind of rest where we choose to soften our stiff necks, allowing Him to bend back our heads in order to do in us and for us what only His words can do. This rest is surrender.

The life of faith is a life of abiding and rest. As the vineyard is silent, no sound of strain or effort on the part of the branches, we are called to abandon self-effort as we surrender to God's presence and voice. Faith doesn't operate by trying hard to believe. Faith operates by connecting and receiving. Faith operates by remaining on the altar. We let the Gardener prune. We let the High Priest cut and pierce. We enter into God's place of rest. With confidence, we draw near.

> "Since then we have a great high priest who has passed through the heavens, Jesus, the Son of God, let us hold fast our confession. For we do not have a high priest who is unable to sympathize with our weaknesses, but one who in every respect has been tempted as we are, yet without sin. Let us then with confidence draw near to the throne of grace, that we may receive mercy and find grace to help in time of need." (Hebrews 4:14–16)

Remain

The only thing a branch needs to do to be successful is remain connected to the vine. This is the root meaning of the word *abide*. When observing a literal grapevine, it is immediately apparent a branch doesn't actually have an option when it comes to remaining. The branch is attached and has no will about the issue.

With humans things are different. The verb *abide* is active, meaning this is something I must do, not something done to me. The verb is imperative, meaning it is a command I am expected to obey. It's difficult to conceive of a branch actively obeying the command to remain attached to the vine, receiving from the vine all it needs.

But in this passage, Jesus clearly intends us to actively choose, as branches, to abide in the vine.

The command to abide implies it is something we should choose; therefore, it is something we can choose, and therefore something we might not choose. The consequences of choosing not to abide are severe.

"If anyone does not abide in me he is thrown away like a branch and withers; and the branches are gathered, thrown into the fire, and burned." (John 15:6)

The essential nature and source of fruitfulness is clear. Every believer lives with the day-to-day choice regarding whether he or she will remain engaged with Jesus' presence and voice, or instead look to some other source of life, significance, identity, provision, or value. Perseverance (often translated *patient endurance*) is key. All of us know through our own experience that although our status with God is secure (due to the finished work of Christ), our experience of His presence and voice can vary greatly, depending upon what we choose to be aware of and upon whom we choose to rely. This is the clearest application of Jesus' command that we abide.

What Do You Hear?
Walk out into the vineyard of your life. Listen. What do you hear? Is your life in God characterized by the sounds

of self-effort and the noise of self-reliance? Or is there a quiet peace, a soundless rest and trust? If striving rather than rest, performance rather than intimate connection, earning rather than receiving marks your relationship with God, then it's time for a change.

Repent. Turn, not from bad behavior to good, but rather from self-effort to surrender. Cease from your own works. Rest in His finished work. Turn your attention, focus and awareness to the reality of Jesus' nearness, goodness, and power. Turn your affections toward Him. Now, just stay there. Rest there. If your gaze gets averted from Him, simply renew your focus and continue. Keep going. Remain. Trust. Receive.

Abide.

12

What Do I Do?

"So also faith by itself, if it does not have works, is dead." (James 2:17)

Where Do I Go From Here?

Much space within these pages has been given to addressing ideas that might seem somewhat abstract. How does God transform us? Why is it important to hear God's voice? Why must we learn to see *here* from the perspective of *there*, and *now* from the perspective of *then*? What is faith? What does it mean to abide in Christ?

Hopefully, working through these ideas has been a catalyst for change. Even the act of reading and thinking about these kinds of things can itself be an expression of living faith. But at some point, it is necessary to get very practical regarding what should be done.

Much of what I suggest will not be new. In fact, some of what I suggest you will instantly recognize, because you are already doing it. I don't want these practical instructions to just offer something different to do, but rather a new way to approach some of the things you're already doing.

Because these instructions are about how you approach what you do, there is a danger they will still seem abstract. They are not. There is an external *doing*. There is an internal *doing*. How we do things internally significantly impacts what we do externally. Thinking is an action. Surrender is a choice, and therefore also an action. External behavior follows our internal behavior.

> *"How we do things internally significantly impacts what we do externally. "*

I also intend, where possible, to give very definite steps where key behaviors will be helpful in the process. Observable behavior is not unimportant; it is just not the starting place for change.

Take Ownership of Your Focus

"Finally, brothers, whatever is true, whatever is honorable, whatever is just, whatever is pure, whatever

is lovely, whatever is commendable, if there is any excellence, if there is anything worthy of praise, think about these things." (Philippians 4:8)

In a sense, I am concluding my book in similar fashion to the manner in which Paul concluded his epistle to the church in Philippi. Paul instructs the believers to choose what they are going to think about, to choose their focus. Evidently, there is a way of thinking that is helpful and a way of thinking that is not. But it is the assumption underlying this instruction that captures me. Paul, in asking me to be intentional about the way I think, must assume this is something I can do.

What do I do?

Take ownership of my thought life.

Sounds simple enough, doesn't it? The instruction itself is not difficult to comprehend, but the underlying assumption is completely counter-cultural. There is a pervasive passivity in most people in our time. Many assume their thought life is something that happens to them, rather than something they have control over. I think there is a primary reason for this.

If we are passive in our thought life, then our thought life will be out of control. If I do not manage my internal focus, I will be managed by it. If I do not own my internal reality, then very likely someone or something else will. If I spend enough time in this passive experience, where my thought world rules over me instead of being ruled by me, then this experience will likely define my boundaries. Content to sit within the cage, I assume the door must be locked. I don't know the gate is unlocked because I've never tried to open it; I've never experienced anything different. But if I try the gate, I will certainly discover it is unlocked. My thought life is something I can choose.

Paul would not tell me to think about certain kinds of things to the exclusion of other kinds of things if it were not so. He assumes this is a choice I can make. I must take ownership of my internal world. This scope of ownership encompasses three areas: my attention, my affection, and my desires. I am responsible for where I aim my awareness, where I direct my emotions, and what I choose to pursue as my source. My will in these matters is not something that happens to me passively. I have a will. This assumes volition is something I have. This assumes there is a *me* that has it. My capacity to choose what I do with my attention, affection, and desire is a weapon I must wield. If I do not take ownership of my attention, affection, and desires, then they will take ownership of me. There is no third option.

Stop being a victim.

You are too powerful to succumb to a victim mentality. This is the first thing you must do.

Lest you grow concerned I mean all this in some kind of humanistic man-centered way, let me be clear: it is essential that you learn to use your will to yield to God and abandon self-reliance and self-focus. Your will was made for surrender.

Much of the emphasis of scripture regards God's desire to be first in our lives. Where should I place my attention? Upon His presence and voice. Where should I place my affections? Upon His goodness and love. Where should I direct my desires? Upon Him as my sole source of security, identity, value, and provision, first of all.

This is essentially what Paul is challenging us to do. It is what he is assuming we are able to do. We can truly experience God's presence and voice in a transforming way as we grow in our revelation of His goodness and love, receiving from Him all we need.

So, what do I do?

First, take ownership of the reality that you *can* choose your focus. It's really one of the few things you actually can control.

It might help to pray aloud something like this:

*Jesus, today I choose to renounce passivity in the area of my attention, affection, and desires. I confess I've been passive. Would you forgive me for this? (**Wait for Him to answer you!**) Today I choose Your presence and voice as the focus of my attention. Today I choose Your goodness and love as the focus of my affection. Today I choose You as my ultimate source of identity, value, significance, security, and provision. I*

acknowledge You have charged me with the responsi-
bility of exercising dominion over my internal world.
Today I exercise this power by surrendering fully to
You. It is what I am made for.

Meditate on Scripture

- **Meditation is Biblical**

The spiritual practice of meditation has been mostly neglected by the people of God, and has instead been counterfeited by practitioners of *Eastern* categories of religion and spirituality. Many Christ followers in the West shy away from this practice because the word *meditation* has taken on a New Age connotation. It's time for us to reclaim this very Biblical practice. The following list is by no means exhaustive, but it is representative of the way scripture speaks of the practice of meditation:

"This Book of the Law shall not depart from your
mouth, but you shall meditate on it day and night, so
that you may be careful to do according to all that is
written in it. For then you will make your way pros-
perous, and then you will have good success." (Joshua
1:8)

"Let the words of my mouth and the meditation of
my heart be acceptable in your sight, O Lord, my rock

and my redeemer." (Psalm 19:14)

"We have thought on your steadfast love, O God, in the midst of your temple." (Psalm 48:9)

"My mouth shall speak wisdom; the meditation of my heart shall be understanding." (Psalm 49:3)

"When I remember you upon my bed, and meditate on you in the watches of the night." (Psalm 63:6)

"I said, 'Let me remember my song in the night; let me meditate in my heart.' Then my spirit made a diligent search." (Psalm 77:6)

"I will ponder all your work, and meditate on your mighty deeds." (Psalm 77:12)

"May my meditation be pleasing to him, for I rejoice in the Lord." (Psalm 104:34)

"I will meditate on your precepts and fix my eyes on your ways." (Psalm 119:15)

"I have more understanding than all my teachers, for your testimonies are my meditation." (Psalm 119:99)

"My eyes are awake before the watches of the night, that I may meditate on your promise." (Psalm 119:148)

- **What is Meditation?**

The Hebrew word translated *meditation* has two roots. The first root means to mutter or speak in a low voice. The second means to consider something inwardly or to be occupied with an idea. Meditation therefore involves the focus of my thoughts and words upon a particular idea. In scripture, we see that the object of our meditation is scripture (the Law, His precepts, etc.), the deeds or works of God (His testimonies, His mighty acts in scripture, the works one has personally experienced in life, etc.), or the attributes of God's nature and character (His goodness, love, etc.).

- **Everyone Knows How to Meditate**

Anyone who has struggled with either fear or lust knows how to meditate, inwardly considering scenarios, ideas, and images in ways that powerfully affect and shape our inner world. Most, however, have not learned to intentionally harness this capacity in the manner it was designed.

- **How to Meditate**

1. Memorize a phrase or verse from the Bible. Though

you can choose an attribute of God or consider a story from your own life when God demonstrated His faithfulness and power, I find it is best to begin with a particular section of scripture. Start with a short verse or phrase that speaks of who God is (His goodness, nearness, or power, for instance) or who I am in Christ. (Psalm 139:7-9; Romans 8:14-17; Ephesians 1:3-4 and 2:4-6 are a few of the verses I keep coming back to over and over again.)

2. Choose a time. The Bible speaks of meditating all day—morning and evening, day and night. There's no bad time to meditate. If you're a beginner, you shouldn't start with the *all day* goal. I recommend setting aside 20 minutes toward the beginning of your day. It has been my experience that setting aside a particular time for focused meditation actually affects the occupation of my thoughts throughout the day.

3. Choose a place. Find a quiet place, free from distraction—if it's aesthetically pleasant and peaceful for you, even better. Calm is important, and if your environment contributes to this it will be helpful. At the very least, locate a spot that doesn't work against you.

4. Choose a posture. No, you don't have to sit cross-legged on the floor with your hands in a particular position. You do, however, need to find a position you can maintain without movement for 20 minutes. Avoid

slouching, crossing one leg over the other, or things that will require you to shift positions frequently because of their effect on your circulation. I find it helpful to sit in a comfortable chair (not a recliner) with both feet flat on the floor. Sit up straight, and rest your hands palm down on your legs. There is nothing special about sitting in this position other than it allows you to not be distracted by how you're sitting.

5. Turn your inward focus upon God's presence. Jesus promised He would never leave you. 2 Corinthians 3:16 tells us when we turn to the Lord, the veil is removed (revelation occurs). Simply choose to be aware God is with you, and choose to be aware of nothing else. You might find it helpful to breathe deeply. Meditation is an act of the mind *and* body.

6. Bring to mind the verse or phrase from scripture you desire to meditate on. Begin to repeatedly rehearse this phrase or verse in your mind. As you do so, maintain your awareness of God's presence.

7. Once you are quiet and fully occupied with both God's presence and the truth of scripture, begin to speak that phrase or verse from scripture repeatedly. No need to do it loudly or dramatically. Remember, the root word means to mutter quietly. You are now meditating on scripture!

Study the Bible

Most Christians know they ought to study the Bible. Many of those don't really know how. Here are a few thoughts that will hopefully help to point you in the right direction.

- **Read for the big picture.**

The Bible is essentially the story of Creation, Redemption, and New Creation. Reading a few verses or even a couple of chapters won't give you the 30,000-foot view you need of this epic narrative. It's important to make the effort to take in large chunks of the Bible in a short amount of time.

The Bible contains 1,189 chapters. Many Bible reading programs are based around reading three to four chapters daily so you can get all the way through the Bible in one year. This is NOT what I'm talking about. I'm talking about working through the entire book of Genesis in a couple of days (50 chapters), or the first five books in a week, or all four gospels in three days. You don't have to sustain this kind of pace all the time, but it's important that you regularly zoom out to take in broad, sweeping sections of the Bible in compressed time frames. There really isn't a better way to get a feel for the big picture. I use an mp3 audio Bible to accomplish this. You'd be amazed how many chapters you can take in just while driving.

- **Dig deep into short passages.**

This has several components. When I want to focus in on a single chapter or shorter passage, I begin by reading through it slowly, multiple times, in order to build familiarity. This part of the process might take several days. I will often take a single key verse or phrase from the passage and commit it to memory. I do this so I can meditate on the passage. Meditation is an essential part of the process. You can learn correct information from scripture without meditation, but meditation is a key to growing in revelation.

Next, you will want to get some good Bible study software. I use Logos. There are several other software packages available for purchase within various price ranges. E-Sword is a powerful program you can download for free. There are also several web-based tools. Most programs offer online tutorials. You will learn much about how to study simply by watching those. Begin by learning to use commentaries, word study tools, and theological dictionaries.

- **Read books by other students of the Bible.**

Don't just read easy books. Find books by authors who will stretch you, who have done their own homework and don't merely share their conclusions, but share their process. Read authors who interact with scripture in their writing and give you a glimpse into their own approach to study. One way to find these authors is to look through the bibliography of some of the books you've already read and benefited from. Learning to read the writers your favorite authors read is a great way to expand your horizons.

- **Teach someone else.**

Teach a Sunday School class, or a small group Bible Study. Teach your own children. Take a friend to coffee and ask if you can share a few ideas from scripture you've been looking at these days. It doesn't have to be a formal setting. My point is teaching is a great catalyst for learning. The process of articulating an explanation really helps to solidify ideas and concepts.

- **Apply what you've learned** (this is the most important one!).

Do the things the Bible tells you to do. Live the life you see modeled by those who follow God in the pages of the Bible. Do they hear God's voice? Then listen. Do they pray for the sick? Then heal. Do they grow in kindness and service? Then be nice. A merely academic approach to scripture that doesn't result in revelation and application is of very little value, if any at all; often, it's actually harmful. Faith always leads to relationship with Jesus. Since Jesus is King, relationship with Jesus always results in increasing obedience. Don't just be a hearer or a reader. Be a doer.

Engage Your Imagination

In Chapter 4, I introduced the idea of the importance of our imagination in the Christian life. More than just a place of childhood make-believe, our imagination is designed by God to be a place of inward sight, sound, smell, touch, and taste. It is the inward movie theater where God speaks to us in dreams and visions. It is the primary arena where we experience God's presence and voice.

Though many have engaged the power of imagination in partnership with lust or fear, few are intentional about using their inner capacity to see the way it was intended.

"If then you have been raised with Christ, seek the things that are above, where Christ is, seated at the right hand of God. Set your minds on things that are above, not on things that are on earth. For you have died, and your life is hidden with Christ in God. When Christ who is your life appears, then you also will appear with him in glory." (Colossians 3:1–4)

Set your minds

"Turn your awareness to the sights and sounds of heaven."

on things that are above is not an instruction to think abstract thoughts about theology. It is an invitation and challenge to inwardly experience heavenly reality. Since you are now seated in heaven, turn your awareness to the sights and sounds of heaven. This is a primary strategy to overcoming sin in your life.

"Put to death therefore what is earthly in you: sexual immorality, impurity, passion, evil desire, and covetousness, which is idolatry." (Colossians 3:5)

How do I *put to death* the junk in my life that is incongruent with the life of Christ? By setting my mind on things above.

You can begin to intentionally practice engaging your imagination in two primary settings: corporate worship and private prayer.

• **Engaging Your Imagination in Corporate Worship**

The difference between participating in a song service and joining the host of heaven around God's throne in worship is simply a matter of engaging your inward capacity to see.[1] As you approach times of worship with your brothers and sisters, begin to build the habit of activating the eyes of your heart as part of this experience.

Here's how I often do this:

Enter in through the veil. Picture the veil in the Temple or the Tabernacle, torn from top to bottom as a result of

Jesus' finished work on the cross. I like to picture it as a very tall, thick curtain. I can see the frayed threads and places along the tattered edges of the seam where light from the Throne Room is bursting out as an invitation to enter in with confident reverence.

Insert your hands between the seams and push the veil back and away so you can step inside. Walk on in. Take in the view:

"At once I was in the Spirit, and behold, a throne stood in heaven, with one seated on the throne. And he who sat there had the appearance of jasper and carnelian, and around the throne was a rainbow that had the appearance of an emerald. Around the throne were twenty-four thrones, and seated on the thrones were twenty-four elders, clothed in white garments, with golden crowns on their heads. From the throne came flashes of lightning, and rumblings and peals of thunder, and before the throne were burning seven torches of fire, which are the seven spirits of God, and before the throne there was as it were a sea of glass, like crystal. And around the throne, on each side of the throne, are four living creatures, full of eyes in front and behind: the first living creature like a lion, the second living creature like an ox, the third living creature with the face of a man, and the fourth living creature like an eagle in flight. And the

four living creatures, each of them with six wings, are full of eyes all around and within, and day and night they never cease to say, 'Holy, holy, holy, is the Lord God Almighty, who was and is and is to come!' And whenever the living creatures give glory and honor and thanks to him who is seated on the throne, who lives forever and ever, the twenty-four elders fall down before him who is seated on the throne and worship him who lives forever and ever. They cast their crowns before the throne, saying, 'Worthy are you, our Lord and God, to receive glory and honor and power, for you created all things, and by your will they existed and were created.'" (Revelation 4:2–11)

As you sing with your congregation, envision not just your church auditorium, not just the people around you—see beyond that to the heavenly reality you are entering together. See the emerald rainbow encircling God's throne. See the elders clothed in white leaping from their thrones to fall prostrate before God's glory as they fling their crowns before Him.

Hear the sounds. See the sights. As you sing, hear more than just the sound of your congregation. Join with the elders and the beasts and the heavenly hosts. Join the sounds of heaven. This biblical imagery exists to draw you into a present reality, not just to describe to you a future reality.

- **Engaging Your Imagination in Private Prayer**

I like to meet with Jesus in the den of my grandparents' home.[2] They have both passed away, and that house was sold long ago. But it represents something significant to me. I always felt safe there. There were other places I sometimes felt safe as a child and others where I often felt safe, but this is the place where I always felt safe. Always. I didn't even realize it at the time, but God was teaching me something about His nature in that place, for I am always safe with Him.

When I pray, I often close my eyes and open the eyes of my heart. I can feel the thick carpet of that room underneath my toes. I can hear the sounds, and smell the smells of Grandma in the kitchen baking. I can see Grandpa pushing his lawnmower in neat precise rows up and down their backyard. I sit in this great chair that's soft and comfortable and spins around. Jesus sits right across the room, about five feet away in another chair that's comfy, but doesn't spin like mine. I talk to Him. He talks to me. I could just as easily visit with Him in the Throne Room. Sometimes I do. But most often, we sit in my grandparents' den. I think He likes that place for me, in me, with me. He always has. Sometimes when we visit there, I'm a grown man with children of my own. Sometimes I'm a little boy again, and He talks with me about the things that concern little boys. I need that sometimes.

Find a place to meet with Jesus. Go there often.

If you make a practice of engaging your imagination in corporate worship and prayer, you will begin to develop your capacity to experience God's presence and voice. This place of inward sight, sound, and touch is the most common place to experience His transforming presence and voice. Go there on purpose. Don't remain passive, leaving this arena of visions and dreams to the influence of the transforming presence and voice of things like lust and fear.

Make Identity the Focus

Your circumstances will always tempt you to make them your focus. Managing behavior might seem an enticing path to transformation. Neither of these can help, though.

Who is God? Who are you? Gaining deeper revelation from God in the answers to these questions must remain your constant goal. Answers come through His presence and voice—answers from the perspective of *there*, not *here*, and *then*, not *now*. For who He is and who I am will be clearly seen only from the perspective of heavenly reality, and the New Heaven and Earth to come.

May we all be continually transformed He unveils who He is, where He is, and who and where we are in Him.

Notes

Chapter One

1. Bob Hamp, *Think Differently, Live Differently: Keys to a Life of Freedom* (Fort Worth: Think Differently Press, 2010), 49.

2. Gregory A. Boyd, *Seeing is Believing: Experiencing Jesus through Imaginative Prayer* (Grand Rapids, Baker Books, 2004), 18.

3. *The Matrix*. Dir. Andy Wachowski and Larry Wachowski. Warner Bros. Pictures, 1999, DVD.

Chapter Two

1. K.J. Vanhoozer, C.G. Bartholomew, D.J. Treier, & N.T. Wright, *Dictionary for Theological Interpretation of the Bible* (Grand Rapids, MI: Baker Academic, 2005), 532.

2. F.A. Schaeffer, *The Complete Works of Francis A. Schaeffer: A Christian Worldview, Book 5: The Great Evangelical Disaster.* (Westchester, IL: Crossway Books, 1996).

3. Schaeffer, *Book 2: The Church Before the Watching World, Chapter 1, The Birth of Liberalism.*

4. N.L. Geisler, *Systematic Theology, Volume Two: God, Creation* (Minneapolis, MN: Bethany House Publishers,

2003), 567.

5. Bill Johnson, *When Heaven Invades Earth: A Practical Guide to a Life of Miracles.* (Shippensburg, PA: Destiny Image Publishers, 2003), 120.

Chapter Four

1. Merriam-Webster, *Merriam-Webster's Collegiate Dictionary, (Eleventh ed.),* (Springfield, MA: Merriam-Webster, Inc., 2003).

2. Gregory A. Boyd, *Seeing is Believing, Experiencing Jesus through Imaginative Prayer* (Grand Rapids, Baker Books, 2004), 70.

3. Boyd, 74

4. Dutch Sheets, *Becoming Who You Are, Embracing the Power of Your Identity in Christ* (Bloomington, MN: Bethany House, 2007), 134

Chapter Five

1. N.T. Wright, *The Resurrection of the Son of God* (London: Society for Promoting Christian Knowledge, 2003), 219.

2. N.T. Wright, *After You Believe, Why Christian Character Matters* (New York, NY: Harper One, 2010), 137.

3. Johnson, 55

4. S. Zodhiates, *The Complete Word Study Dictionary: New Testament* (electronic ed.), (Chattanooga, TN: AMG Publishers, 2000).

5. Hamp, 137

6. G.E. Ladd, *The Last Things: An eschatology for Laymen* (Grand Rapids, MI: William B. Eerdmans Publishing Company, 1978), 104.

7. N. T. Wright, *The New Testament and the People of God* (London: Society for Promoting Christian Knowledge, 1992), 299-300.

8. Johnson, 60

Chapter Six

1. John Piper, *Future Grace* (Sisters, OR: Multnomah Publishers, 1995), 373.

Chapter Seven

1. Wright, *The New Testament and the People of God*, 290

2. N. T. Wright, *Jesus and the victory of God* (London: Society for Promoting Christian Knowledge, 1996), 205.

3. Danny Silk, *A Culture of Honor: Sustaining a Supernatural Environment* (Shippensburg, PA: Destiny Image, 2009), 19.

Chapter Eight

1. Johnson, 55

Chapter Nine

1. Sheets, 124

2. Sheets, 41

3. Boyd, 35

Chapter Eleven
1. Piper, 158
2. Willard, Dallas *The divine Conspiracy, Rediscovering Our Hidden Life in God* (New York: Harper One, 1997), 142.
3. Willard, 275
4. Sheets, 198

Chapter Twelve
1. Boyd, 86
2. Boyd, 94